Praise for *How Happiness Happens*

Cook Memorial Public Lib[...]

3 1122 01603 9450

AUG 3 - 2021

W9-CFC-255

"For me and my family, I've always said that the farm isn't what made us happy. Instead, I believe it was everything that happened on our way to the farm . . . and it's because of that journey that we are the people we are today. I love Max Lucado, I love his family, and I love the perspective he shares in *How Happiness Happens*. If you're looking for a wake-up call or a dose of modern-day wisdom, read this book. In fact, read all of his books—you'll be glad you did."

—CHIP GAINES, MAGNOLIA COFOUNDER

"In a world where happiness has become fickle and fleeting, Max takes us back to Jesus' path to happiness that is rooted in true joy and loving others. *How Happiness Happens* will challenge you to focus less on yourself and your circumstances, and more on our good God—the true source of our joy."

—CHRISTINE CAINE, BESTSELLING AUTHOR;
FOUNDER, A21 AND PROPEL WOMEN

"In a generation wrestling with comparison and desperately searching for joy, Max beautifully communicates the simplicity of happiness in his new book *How Happiness Happens*. The call to kindness and thoughtful intention is extended to us all. This is a timely message that we all need!"

—KIM WALKER-SMITH, JESUS CULTURE

"Max has done it again! This book is packed with simple reminders of how small acts of kindness can pay massive dividends in our own happiness and then impact the lives of those we come into contact with on a daily basis."

—DAVID GREEN, CEO, HOBBY LOBBY STORES, INC.

"There's a reason my friend Max Lucado is one of the bestselling Christian authors of all time! His words touch our hearts with a gentle whisper that in time becomes a roaring waterfall of the Father's freedom and love. *How Happiness Happens* will delight and awaken you, leading you to a greater peace and purpose than you've ever known before."

—LOUIE GIGLIO, PASSION CITY CHURCH, PASSION CONFERENCES,
AUTHOR OF *NOT FORSAKEN* AND *GOLIATH MUST FALL*

"Max Lucado's books always look into our hearts, our souls, and our behavior toward one another. His latest book *How Happiness Happens* is no different as he teaches that doing for others makes our hearts feel good and brings us happiness. He uses Scripture in teaching how to bring joy and happiness to those around us. In one of the chapters, Max mentions that 'doing good does good for the doer' and I could not agree more."

—DELILAH, RADIO PERSONALITY AND AUTHOR

"Max Lucado, one of the leading Christian writers of our time, has written a wonderful book about one of life's most important subjects: happiness. I have long argued that the happy make the world better and the unhappy make it worse. Therefore, this book can make the world better. I hope millions read it. And while it is written from a Christian's perspective, anyone of any faith—or of no faith—will greatly benefit from it. I am a Jew, and I loved it."

—DENNIS PRAGER, NATIONALLY SYNDICATED RADIO TALK SHOW HOST AND *NEW YORK TIMES* BESTSELLING AUTHOR

"I was a college student home from school for the summer and working part-time at my church. My dad, the pastor, encouraged me to begin my mornings by having a daily quiet time. In addition to my Bible, he handed me a stack of books by Max Lucado. I read them one by one, cover to cover. Max's gifted storytelling and powerful teachings ministered to me then, and his books are still accompanying my daily quiet times today. I've been challenged greatly by *How Happiness Happens* and its powerful chapter by chapter reminder that the way we love others just might cause a much needed 'quiet revolution of joy.' Thanks Max, you keep speaking to me!"

–MATTHEW WEST, DOVE AWARD WINNER AND FOUR-TIME GRAMMY NOMINEE

"As a leader who coaches others to fully embrace their calling, I have learned firsthand how elusive happiness can be if separated from a servant's heart and a generous spirit. In typical Max Lucado brilliance, *How Happiness Happens* sets our assumptions on end and lovingly invites us to live more fully like Jesus. In the process, we will find what we've been searching for all along—true happiness."

—KADI COLE, LEADERSHIP CONSULTANT AND AUTHOR OF *DEVELOPING FEMALE LEADERS*, KADICOLE.COM

"The genius of Max is his ability to use God's Word in an expository way, so we can easily apply it to our lives. The book *How Happiness Happens* is another example of how God speaks through Max."

—Lance Barrow, coordinating producer, *Golf CBS Sports*

"Wow, the world is searching for something: contentment, happiness, joy, or whatever. Max Lucado reminds us that where we look shapes what we find. As Max always does, he explains what we need to know about happiness and then points us in the right direction. You will be blessed as you understand happiness better!"

—Ed Stetzer, Billy Graham Center, Wheaton College

HOW
Happiness
Happens

ALSO BY MAX LUCADO

INSPIRATIONAL

3:16
A Gentle Thunder
A Love Worth Giving
And the Angels
Were Silent
Anxious for Nothing
Because of Bethlehem
Before Amen
Begin Again
Come Thirsty
Cure for the Common Life
Facing Your Giants
Fearless
Glory Days
God Came Near
Grace
Great Day Every Day
He Chose the Nails
He Still Moves Stones
How Happiness Happens
In the Eye of the Storm
In the Grip of Grace
It's Not About Me
Jesus
Just Like Jesus
Max on Life
More to Your Story
Next Door Savior
No Wonder They Call
Him the Savior
On the Anvil
Outlive Your Life
Six Hours One Friday
The Applause of Heaven
The Great House of God
Traveling Light
Unshakable Hope
When Christ Comes

When God Whispers
Your Name
You Are Never Alone
You'll Get Through This

FICTION

Christmas Stories
Miracle at the Higher
Grounds Café
The Christmas Candle

BIBLES (GENERAL EDITOR)

The Lucado Encouraging
Word Bible
Children's Daily
Devotional Bible
Grace for the Moment
Daily Bible
The Lucado Life
Lessons Study Bible

CHILDREN'S BOOKS

A Max Lucado
Children's Treasury
Do You Know I
Love You, God?
God Always Keeps
His Promises
God Forgives Me,
and I Forgive You
God Listens When I Pray
Grace for the Moment:
365 Devotions for Kids
Hermie, a Common
Caterpillar
I'm Not a Scaredy Cat
Itsy Bitsy Christmas
Just in Case You

Ever Wonder
Lucado Treasury of
Bedtime Prayers
One Hand, Two Hands
Thank You, God,
for Blessing Me
Thank You, God,
for Loving Me
The Boy and the Ocean
The Crippled Lamb
The Oak Inside the Acorn
The Tallest of Smalls
You Are Mine
You Are Special

YOUNG ADULT BOOKS

3:16
It's Not About Me
Make Every Day Count
Wild Grace
You Were Made to
Make a Difference

GIFT BOOKS

Fear Not Promise Book
For the Tough Times
God Thinks You're
Wonderful
Grace for the Moment
Grace Happens Here
Happy Today
His Name Is Jesus
Let the Journey Begin
Live Loved
Mocha with Max
Safe in the
Shepherd's Arms
This Is Love
You Changed My Life

HOW
Happiness
Happens

FINDING **LASTING JOY** IN A WORLD OF COMPARISON,
DISAPPOINTMENT, AND UNMET EXPECTATIONS

MAX LUCADO

COOK MEMORIAL LIBRARY
413 N. MILWAUKEE AVE.
LIBERTYVILLE, ILLINOIS 60048
MAY 0 5 2021

THOMAS NELSON
Since 1798

© 2019 Max Lucado

All rights reserved. No portion of this book may be reproduced, stored in a retrieval system, or transmitted in any form or by any means—electronic, mechanical, photocopy, recording, scanning, or other—except for brief quotations in critical reviews or articles, without the prior written permission of the publisher.

Published in Nashville, Tennessee, by Thomas Nelson. Thomas Nelson is a registered trademark of HarperCollins Christian Publishing, Inc.

Thomas Nelson titles may be purchased in bulk for educational, business, fund-raising, or sales promotional use. For information, please email SpecialMarkets@ThomasNelson.com.

Any Internet addresses, phone numbers, or company or product information printed in this book are offered as a resource and are not intended in any way to be or to imply an endorsement by Thomas Nelson, nor does Thomas Nelson vouch for the existence, content, or services of these sites, phone numbers, companies, or products beyond the life of this book.

Unless otherwise noted, Scripture quotations are taken from the New King James Version®. © 1982 by Thomas Nelson. Used by permission. All rights reserved.

Other Scripture references are from the following sources: American Standard Version (ASV). Amplified® Bible (AMP), copyright © 1954, 1958, 1962, 1964, 1965, 1987 by The Lockman Foundation. Used by permission. (www.Lockman.org). Contemporary English Version (CEV), copyright © 1991, 1992, 1995 by American Bible Society. Used by permission. English Standard Version (ESV), © 2001 by Crossway Bibles, a division of Good News Publishers. The Expanded Bible (EXB). © 2011 by Thomas Nelson. Used by permission. All rights reserved. Good News Translation in Today's English Version—Second Edition (GNT). Copyright 1992 by American Bible Society. Used by permission. *The Jerusalem Bible* (JERUSALEM BIBLE). © 1966 by Darton Longman & Todd Ltd. and Doubleday and Company Ltd. King James Version (KJV). *The Message* (THE MESSAGE). Copyright © by Eugene H. Peterson 1993, 1994, 1995, 1996, 2000, 2001, 2002. Used by permission of Tyndale House Publishers, Inc. New American Standard Bible® (NASB, 1977). Copyright © 1960, 1962, 1963, 1968, 1971, 1972, 1973, 1975, 1977 by The Lockman Foundation. Used by permission. (www.Lockman.org). New American Standard Bible® (NASB). Copyright © 1960, 1962, 1963, 1968, 1971, 1972, 1973, 1975, 1977, 1995 by The Lockman Foundation. Used by permission. (www.Lockman.org). New Century Version® (NCV). © 2005 by Thomas Nelson. Used by permission. All rights reserved. Holy Bible, New International Version®, NIV® (NIV). Copyright © 1973, 1978, 1984, 2011 by Biblica, Inc.™ Used by permission of Zondervan. All rights reserved worldwide. www.zondervan.com. *Holy Bible*, New Living Translation (NLT). © 1996, 2004, 2007, 2013, 2015 by Tyndale House Foundation. Used by permission of Tyndale House Publishers, Inc., Carol Stream, Illinois 60188. All rights reserved. New Scofield Reference Bible (NSRB). Copyright © 1967 by Oxford University Press, Inc. J. B. Phillips: THE NEW TESTAMENT IN MODERN ENGLISH, Revised Edition (PHILLIPS). © J. B. Phillips 1958, 1960, 1972. Used by permission of Macmillan Publishing Co., Inc. Revised Standard Version of the Bible (RSV), copyright 1946, 1952, and 1971 National Council of the Churches of Christ in the United States of America. Used by permission. All rights reserved. *The Living Bible* (TLB). Copyright © 1971. Used by permission of Tyndale House Publishers, Inc., Carol Stream, Illinois 60188. All rights reserved. *The Voice*™ (THE VOICE). © 2012 by Ecclesia Bible Society. Used by permission. All rights reserved. Note: Italics in quotations from The Voice are used to "indicate words not directly tied to the dynamic translation of the original language" but that "bring out the nuance of the original, assist in completing ideas, and . . . provide readers with information that would have been obvious to the original audience" (The Voice, preface).

ISBN: 978-0-7180-9613-7 (HC)
ISBN: 978-0-7180-7425-8 (IE)
ISBN: 978-0-7180-9647-2 (Ebook)
ISBN: 978-1-4041-1444-9 (CU)
ISBN: 978-0-7180-7427-2 (TP)

Library of Congress Control Number: 2019943260

Printed in the United States of America

21 22 23 24 25 LSC 6 5 4 3 2 1

For Jim Barker

For twenty-five years you've taught me, pastored
me, and attempted to fix my golf swing.
Two out of three ain't bad.
Thank you, friend.

Contents

Acknowledgments

A resounding hip, hip, hooray for . . .

Karen Hill and Liz Heaney: invaluable editors who know how to persuade this stubborn donkey of an author to take another step up the hill.

Carol Bartley: incomparable copy editor who is to errors what a sherlock is to clues. Not a single one gets past you.

Steve and Cheryl Green: friends and partners for more than forty years. We cherish the relationship.

The HCCP team of standard-setting superstars: Mark Schoenwald, David Moberg, Brian Hampton, Mark Glesne, Jessalyn Foggy, Janene MacIvor, and Laura Minchew.

Brand team managers Greg and Susan Ligon: every author needs a "Greg and Susan," especially this one.

———

Dave Treat: thank you for your steadfast prayers for this manuscript and many others.

Administrative assistants Janie Padilla and Margaret Mechinus: for all I know that you do and the much more I don't know about, thank you!

The staff and elders of the Oak Hills Church: you are faithful, steadfast, and a lot of fun.

Ed and Becky Blakey: thank you for your over-the-top hospitality and the use of the ED-itorial writing room.

Brett, Jenna, Rosie, and Max; Andrea; Jeff and Sara: our splendid family. I could not possibly love you more.

And Denalyn, my dear wife. How does happiness happen? Simple. Marry Denalyn. It sure worked for me. I love you.

1

The Unexpected Door to Joy

It's 6:00 a.m. in Hamilton, Bermuda. Ninety-two-year-old Johnny Barnes stands on the edge of a roundabout and waves at people as they drive past. He's been here since before 4:00 a.m. He'll be here until 10:00 a.m. He's not asking for money or begging for food. He's not protesting, complaining, picketing, or loitering.

He's making people happy.

He wears a straw hat and a salty beard. His eyes are bright, teeth white, and skin leathery and dark. The years have bent his back and slowed his step. But they haven't siphoned his joy. He waves with both hands extended in front of him. His wrists turn from side to side as if he were adjusting the volume on a soundboard.

He pulls back his right hand to retrieve a kiss and blow it in the direction of a taxi driver or commuter.

"I love you!" he shouts. "I'll love you forever!" "Hello, there, darlin'. I love you!"

And they love him! Bermudans call him Mr. Happy Man. They route their morning commute to see him. If Johnny's not standing in his spot, people call the radio station to check on him. If he happens to miss acknowledging some commuters, they often circle the roundabout until he waves at them. One morning a cranky woman determined not to make eye contact with him. She wanted to wallow in her bad mood. But she ended up looking his way. When he smiled, she smiled.

Another sour attitude bit the dust.

Johnny's philosophy is simple. "We human beings gotta learn how to love one another. One of the greatest joys that can come to an individual is when you're doing something and helping others."[1]

Wouldn't you love to meet a person like him?

Better still, wouldn't you like to be like him?

How long has it been since you felt a level of contagious, infectious, unflappable, unstoppable happiness? Maybe your answer is "I feel that way all the time." If so, God bless you. (And consider passing on this book to someone who needs it.) For many, perhaps most of us, the answer is "Well, it's been a while. I used to be happy, but then life took its toll."

"The disease took my health."

"The economy took my job."

"The jerk took my heart."

And as a result something pilfered our happiness. It can seem such a fragile thing, this joy. Here one day. Tomorrow scattered by the winds of a storm.

Still we keep searching for it, longing for it, this sense of contentment and well-being. Worldwide, people profess that happiness is their most cherished goal.[2] The most popular class in the three-century history of Yale University is on happiness.[3] Magazine covers promise everything from sexual happiness to financial contentment. I googled "happy hour," and in one second seventy-five million options invited my click.

Marketing companies get this. Television commercials make grand promises: Want to be happy? Buy our hand cream. Want some joy? Sleep on this mattress. Desire a dose of delight? Eat at this restaurant, drive this car, wear this dress. Nearly every advertising strategy portrays the image of a joy-filled person, even the advertisement for Preparation H. Before using the product the guy scowls as he sits. Afterward he is the image of joy. Perhaps the *H* stands for *happy*?

Happiness. Everyone craves it.

And everyone benefits from it. Happy people enjoy higher odds of a strong marriage, lower odds of divorce, and superior work performance. They are also healthier, resulting from a bolstered immune system.[4] In one study researchers found a correlation between happiness and fatter pocketbooks.[5] An analysis of twenty-five studies indicated that happy people are more effective leaders than Debbie Downers.[6] Happiness, it turns out, helps everyone.

But fewer people are finding it. Only one-third of Americans surveyed said they were happy. In the nine-year history of the Harris Poll Survey of American Happiness, the highest index was 35 percent. This means a cloud of perpetual grayness overshadows two out of three people.[7] Smiles are in short supply. By some estimates clinical depression is ten times more rampant now than it was a century ago.[8] The World Health Organization forecasts that by the year 2020 "depression will become the second leading cause of disease worldwide."[9]

It used to be that older people were happier. People in their sixties and seventies generally scored higher in the areas of contentment and appreciation of life. That has changed. Age does not seem to bring the satisfaction it once did.[10]

How can this be? Education is accessible to most. We've made advancements in everything from medicine to technology, yet 66 percent of us can't find an adequate reason to check the yes box on the happiness questionnaire.

Are genetics to blame? Not to the degree one might think. Heredity may influence as much as 50 percent of our disposition. Even if this number is accurate, that leaves the other 50 percent under our purview.[11]

What's up? How do we explain the gloom? While the answers are varied and complex, among them must be this idea: we are using the wrong door.

The oft-used front door to happiness is the one described by the advertising companies: acquire, retire, and aspire to drive faster, dress trendier, and drink more. Happiness depends on what you hang in your closet, park in your garage, mount on your trophy wall, deposit in your bank account, experience in your bedroom, wear on your wedding finger, or serve at your dining table. Happiness happens when you lose the weight, get the date, find the mate, or discover your fate. It's wide, this front door to happiness.

Yet for all its promise it fails to deliver.

In a classic study psychologists determined that recent winners of the Illinois State Lottery were no happier than recent accident victims who were consequently disabled. The two groups were asked to "rate the amount of pleasure they got from everyday activities: small but enjoyable things like chatting with a friend, watching TV, eating breakfast, laughing at a joke, or receiving a compliment. When the researchers analyzed their results, they found that the recent accident victims reported gaining more happiness from these everyday pleasures than the lottery winners."[12]

Even the thrill of winning the lottery wears off.

More money makes truly poor people happier insofar as it relieves pressure from everyday life—getting enough to eat, having a place to live, affording medical care. But once people reach the middle-class income level, even big financial gains don't yield much, if any, increase in happiness.[13] Americans who earn more than $10 million annually report a happiness level only slightly higher than the blue-collar workers they employ.[14] As one Harvard professor said, "We think money will bring lots of happiness for a long time, and actually it brings a little happiness for a short time."[15]

We've all seen happy peasants and miserable millionaires, right?

There is another option. It requires no credit card, monthly mortgage, or stroke of fortune. It demands no airline tickets or hotel reservations. It stipulates no PhD, MD, or blue-blood pedigree. Age, ethnicity, and gender are not factors. Balmy climates, blue skies, and Botox are not mandated. No resources for psychoanalysis, plastic surgery, or hormone therapy? No problem. You don't have to change jobs, change cities, change looks, or change neighborhoods.

But you might need to change doors.

The motto on the front door says "Happiness happens when you get." The sign on the lesser-used back door counters "Happiness happens when you give."

Doing good does good for the doer.

Research bears this out.

When volunteers were put in a functional MRI scanner and were told they would be giving some of their money to charity, the areas of their brains associated with pleasure—like food and sex—lit up like Christmas trees. Giving to help others triggers dopamine.[16] (New fundraising slogan perhaps?)

In another study a team of social psychologists distilled happiness factors into eight common denominators. Two of the first three involve helping others. Happy, contented people "devote a great amount of time to their family and friends, nurturing and enjoying those relationships." And "they are often the first to offer a helping hand to co-workers and passers-by."[17]

Seeking joy? Do good for someone else. A tender example of this truth came my way just today. I met with a husband and daughter to plan the funeral of the wife and mother. Patty was the picture of unselfishness. We tried to imagine how many kids she had hugged, diapers she had changed, children she had taught, and hearts she had encouraged. To see her smile was to see springtime thaw the winter ice.

Three months ago a brain condition had left her unable to speak, partially paralyzed, and living in a rehabilitation center. Her spirits sank so low she did not want to eat and had trouble sleeping. One evening her daughter had an idea. She placed her mother in a wheelchair and rolled her from room to room, looking for people who needed encouragement. It didn't take long.

Though unable to speak, Patty could touch and pray. So she did both. She patted other patients and then placed her hand on their hearts and bowed her head. For the better part of the evening, she touched and prayed her way through the rehab center. That night her appetite returned, and she slept peacefully.

The words of Jesus are spot-on: "It is more blessed to give than to receive" (Acts 20:35). Because when you do, it has a boomerang effect. Happiness happens when we give it away.

This is such great news. You can't control your genetics. You aren't in charge of the weather, the traffic, or the occupant of the White House. But you can always increase the number of smiles on our planet. You can lower the anger level in your city. You—yes, you—can help people to sleep better, laugh more, hum instead of grumble, walk instead of stumble. You can lighten the load and brighten the day of other human beings. And don't be surprised when you begin to sense a newfound joy yourself. That's what this book is about: the unexpected door to joy.

And standing at the entryway to welcome you is Jesus of Nazareth.

Jesus was accused of much, but he was never ever described as a grump, sourpuss, or self-centered jerk. People didn't groan when he appeared. They didn't duck for cover when he entered the room.

He called them by name.

He listened to their stories.

He answered their questions.

He visited their sick relatives and helped their sick friends.

He fished with fishermen and ate lunch with the little guy and spoke words of resounding affirmation. He went to weddings. He was even placed in charge of the wine list at a wedding. He went to so many parties that he was criticized for hanging out with rowdy people and questionable crowds. Thousands came to hear him. Hundreds chose to follow him. They shut down their businesses and walked away from careers to be with him. His purpose statement read "I came to give life with joy and abundance" (John 10:10 THE VOICE). Jesus was happy and wants us to be the same.

When the angels announced the arrival of the Messiah, they proclaimed "good news of a great joy" (Luke 2:10 RSV), not "bad news of a great duty." Scripture has more than twenty-seven hundred passages that contain words like *joy, happiness, gladness, merriment, pleasure, celebration, cheer, laughter, delight, jubilation, feasting, blessing,* and *exultation.*[18] Our joy level matters to God.

This is no call to naivete or superficial happy talk. Jesus spoke candidly about sin, death, and the needs of the human heart. Yet he did so with hope. He brought joy to the people of first-century Palestine. And he wants to bring joy to the people of this generation, and he has enlisted some special agents of happiness to do the job. You and me.

Not an easy task. The people in our world can be moody, fickle, and stubborn. And that just describes my wife's husband. If we are going to find the joy that comes through giving joy away, we need a plan. We need instruction. No wonder the Bible has so much to say about finding joy in the act of sharing it. The New Testament contains more than fifty "one another" statements, practical principles for making happiness happen. I've condensed them into a list of ten.

1. Encourage one another (1 Thess. 5:11).
2. Bear with one another (Eph. 4:2).
3. Regard one another as more important (Phil. 2:4).
4. Greet one another (Rom. 16:16).
5. Pray for one another (James 5:16).
6. Serve one another (Gal. 5:13).
7. Accept one another (Rom. 15:7).
8. Admonish one another (Col. 3:16).
9. Forgive one another (Eph. 4:32).
10. Love one another (1 John 3:11).

Let's open the door to each of these "one another" passages and embark on a happiness project. I'm thinking you will discover what the Bible teaches and research affirms: doing good does good for the doer.

You and I indwell a lonely planet. Broken hearts populate every office building. Discouragement mummifies countless lives. The world is desperate, yes, desperate, for a cavalry of kindness. We cannot solve every problem in society, but we can bring smiles to a few faces. And who knows? If you brighten your corner of the world and I do the same in mine, a quiet revolution of joy might break out.

2

Gimme Five, Rocky

Therefore encourage one another
and build each other up.

—1 Thessalonians 5:11 niv

My big brother used to pick on me. For Dee no day was complete unless he had made mine miserable. He'd trip me as I entered the room. He'd yank back the covers on my just-made bed. He'd wrestle me to the floor and sit on my chest until I couldn't breathe. When his bike had a flat tire, he'd steal mine. He'd kick me beneath the dinner table, and when I kicked back, he'd feign innocence, and I'd get caught. Thanks to him I learned the meaning of the word *wedgie*. He stole my allowance. He called me a sissy. He threw grass burs at me. His waking thought was *How can I pick on Max?*

But all his cruel antics were offset by one great act of grace. He picked me to play on his baseball team.

Mom had given him baby-brother duty that summer day. He could go to the park if he let me tag along. He groaned but relented. He wasn't about to miss the daily baseball game. We grabbed our bats, hats, and Spalding gloves. We jumped on our bikes and raced to the baseball diamond. By the time we arrived, the place was swarming with kids.

When it came time to pick teams, I took my place behind the others and braced for the worst.

Squad selection is enough to scar the psyche of a young boy. It works like this. Two players, presumably the best athletes, begin calling out names. "I get Johnny." "I get Tommy." "I want Jason." "I'll take Eric."

Johnny, Tommy, Jason, and Eric strut and swagger in the direction of their respective captains and strike the cool-kid pose. They deserve to. They were chosen first.

The winnowing process continues, one by one, until the last kid is standing. That day that kid, I just knew, would have freckles and red hair. On the social ladder of summer baseball, I dangled from the lowest rung.

Everyone else was a middle schooler; I was a third grader. Everyone else could handle a baseball bat. I never got a hit. Everyone else could pitch, catch, and steal bases. I had a rag arm, slow glove, and bricks for feet.

But a miracle happened. When angels discuss mighty acts of divine intervention, this moment makes the list. Along with the stories of the Red Sea opening and the was-dead Lazarus walking is the day my brother chose me. Not first, mind you. But far from last. He still had plenty of good guys from whom to pick. But for a reason known only to him and God above, he chose me.

"I take Max," he announced.

A murmur rippled through the crowd. "Max?" *"Max?"* Had the event been part of a movie, the gaggle would have parted, and the camera would have focused on the little fellow wearing the red hat. My eyes opened watermelon wide.

"Who, me?"

"Yeah, you!" my brother barked as if to downplay his largesse.

I tilted my head to the side, smiled an Elvis smile, swaggered through the sad, pitiful lot of unpicked players, and took my place next to my unexpected hero. In the time it took to say my name, I went from the back of the pack to the front of the line, all because he picked me.

Dee didn't pick me because I was good. He didn't select me for my skill or baseball savvy. He called my name for one reason and one reason only. He was my big brother. And on that day he decided to be a good big brother.

The New Testament has a word for such activity: *encouragement*. "Therefore encourage one another and build each other up" (1 Thess. 5:11 NIV).

God does this. He is "the God who gives endurance and encouragement" (Rom. 15:5 NIV).

So does Jesus. "We pray that our Lord Jesus Christ and God our Father will encourage you and help you always to do and say the right thing" (2 Thess. 2:16–17 CEV).

When Jesus introduced the Holy Spirit to us in John 14–16, he called him the *paraklétos*, the noun form of the very word for encouragement.[1]

Scripture encourages us. "The Scriptures were written to teach and encourage us by giving us hope" (Rom. 15:4 CEV).

The saints in heaven encourage us. "Therefore, since we are surrounded by such a huge crowd of witnesses to the life of faith, let us strip off every weight that slows us down, especially the sin that so easily trips us up. And let us run with endurance the race God has set before us" (Heb. 12:1 NLT). A multitude of God's children is urging us on. Like spectators in the stands, a "crowd of witnesses" applauds from the heavens, calling on us to finish strong.

The Father, the Son, the Holy Spirit, the holy Scriptures, the saints. God places a premium on encouragement.

Encouragement occurs when we "come alongside and call out." At least that is the impression we get from its Greek definition. The noun *paraklēsis* is the combination of *para* (by the side) and *kaleō* (to call).[2]

Jesus modeled this.

Peter was the disciple with the foot-shaped mouth. He was prone to speak too soon and boast too much. Yet Jesus saw something in the heart of this crusty fisherman worth calling forth.

When Jesus came into the region of Caesarea Philippi, He asked His disciples, saying, "Who do men say that I, the Son of Man, am?"

So they said, "Some say John the Baptist, some Elijah, and others Jeremiah or one of the prophets."

He said to them, "But who do you say that I am?"

Simon Peter answered and said, "You are the Christ, the Son of the living God." (Matt. 16:13–16)

Caesarea Philippi sat squarely on the boundary between Israel and the Gentile world. It attracted caravans and pilgrims from as far south as Ethiopia and as far north as modern-day Turkey. As much as any city in ancient Palestine, this was a melting pot of people.

The homespun followers of Jesus might well have gulped at the city's cosmopolitan flair. They would have heard the lure of women and the sounds of taverns and smelled the foreign delicacies. But most of all they would have seen the temples. Religion was to Caesarea Philippi what produce is to a street market. Every type of deity was worshiped there.

It was in this maelstrom of religions and cultures that Jesus asked his followers, "Who do you say that I am?" I hear silence from the disciples. A throat being cleared. A sigh or two or ten. I see eyes lower and shoulders slump and heads duck.

Finally Peter spoke up. We can imagine a long, lingering pause after which he said the most audacious words he, and perhaps anyone, had ever spoken. He looked at the penniless rabbi from Galilee and said, "You are the Christ, the Son of the living God" (Matt. 16:16).

Christ, by definition, means the anointed or chosen one. The Christ, in the Hebrew mind-set, wasn't just head of the class; he was his own class. He wasn't the final word; he was the only Word. Jesus, Peter dared to declare, was the Christ.

Jesus all but jumped for joy at the confession. "Blessed are you, Simon Bar-Jonah" (Matt. 16:17). In modern-day parlance, "Way to go! You're the man! Give me five! You nailed it!" Jesus gave Peter the equivalent of a standing ovation, maybe a chest bump. It's as if he threw both arms around the burly fisherman and squeezed any lingering hesitation out of him.

He even changed the apostle's name. Simon would now be called Peter, a name that is next of kin to *petros* or Rocky. Simon, the man who expressed rock-solid faith, needed a rock-solid name. So Jesus gave it to him.

How do you suppose this burst of affirmation made Peter feel? When his friends began calling him Rocky, when Jesus put an arm around his shoulders and said, "Love you, Rocky," when he dozed off to sleep at night thinking of his new name, Rocky, do you suppose he felt encouraged? Of course he did.

Jesus did to Peter what encouragers do. He summoned the best. He built Peter up. With the skill of rock masons, encouragers stack stones of affirmation and inspiration.

Their efforts pay high dividends. Decades of marriage research led Dr. John Gottman to identify an interesting characteristic of happy couples. Healthy homes enjoy a positive-to-negative ratio of five to one. In other words, for every negative comment or criticism, there are five acts or words of encouragement.[3]

Similar results were found among business teams. One study of effective leadership styles revealed that high-performing teams experienced a positive-to-negative ratio of nearly six positive comments for every nega-tive one. Low-performing teams, conversely, had an average of three negative comments for every positive one.[4]

Intentional encouragement has affected my life. Three years into my role as senior minister of our church, a former senior minister returned, not only to live in our city, but also to serve on our staff. Charles Prince was thirty years my senior, Harvard educated, and a member of the Mensa society. I was in my midthirties, a rookie, and a charter member of the Dense society. The relationship could have been awkward and intimidating, but Charles preempted any stress with a visit to my office, during which he said, "There will be no tension in our relationship. I'm going to be your biggest cheerleader."

He was! For twenty-five years, right until the day he died, I could count on a postsermon pat on the back. "You're getting better every week!" I found that hard to believe, but I always appreciated it.

Such encouragement has a Michelangelo impact on people. The sculptor saw the figure of David within the marble and carved it out. The encourager sees your best self and calls it out, not with a chisel, but with words of affirmation.

Dr. Barbara Fredrickson, author of *Positivity* and a social psy-chologist in North Carolina, asserts that positive emotions increase our awareness, allowing us to see the bigger picture and expand our peripheral vision. By opening up the mind, positive emotions help us strengthen our relationships and even improve our physical health because they increase our energy. In contrast, neutral states tend to limit our mind-sets, and negative emotions contract our mind-sets even more so.[5]

Stated differently, if a soccer coach wants to increase the odds of a player missing another goal, he should get angry and shout at her. If the coach wants the player to return to the game with better vision, he should give her a word of affirmation. "People have a way of becoming what you encourage them to be—not what you nag them to be."[6]

A little boy said these words to his father: "Dad, let's play darts. I'll throw, and you say 'Wonderful!'"

Every person needs to hear a "wonderful." Here is why. A *discouragement* conspiracy is afoot. Companies spend billions of dollars to convince us that we are deficient and inadequate. To sell face cream, they tell us that our faces are wrinkled. To sell new clothes, they pronounce that our clothes are out of fashion. To sell hair color, they must persuade us that our hair is dingy. Marketing companies deploy the brightest minds and deepest pockets of our generation to convince us that we are chubby, smelly, ugly, and out-of-date. We are under attack!

We can relate to the two cows grazing in a pasture when a milk truck drove by. On the side of the truck were the words "pasteurized, homogenized, standardized, vitamin A added." Noticing this, one cow said to the other, "Makes you kind of feel inadequate, doesn't it?"

Inadequacy indwells a billion hearts.

Who is going to tell people the truth? Will you? Will you distribute encouragement to the world? Will you make some happiness happen? Will you call the forgotten kid from the back of the pack to the front? Will you remind humanity that we are made in God's image? That we are chosen, destined, and loved? That God is for us, not against us? That we are in God's hand, in God's plan? Will you go face-to-face with the tidal wave of inadequacy that sucks people out to sea?

Will you reach out to the Tim Scotts of the world? Tim was dealt a bad hand of cards. His parents divorced when he was seven years old. His mother, an African American nursing assistant, worked sixteen hours a day but still couldn't lift her family out of poverty. As a teenager, when many of his friends were discovering video games and girls, Tim served popcorn at the local movie theater. During his break he would hurry across the street to a fast-food restaurant and get fries and water. John Moniz owned the facility. He noticed the repeat customer and asked him why he wasn't buying more food. Tim told him he couldn't afford it.

Moniz considered the plight of this teenage boy. He decided to encourage him. One evening he took a bag of sandwiches across the street. The two struck up a conversation that led to a friendship that led to a mentorship. Moniz learned that Tim was failing several classes at school, so Moniz shared with him life lessons about discipline and responsibility. He conveyed the biblical business principles he was using at his workplace. Most important, Moniz taught his young friend about Jesus.

Tim began eating up all the sandwiches and wisdom that Moniz had to give. The seventeen-year-old began to feel life coming together for him. Then tragedy struck. Moniz, age thirty-seven, died of a pulmonary embolism. Tim was left standing at the graveside of his friend and at a crossroads. Much to his credit he chose to put the lessons Moniz had taught him to good use. He wrote a new purpose statement for his life. His mission? To have a positive effect on one billion people.

Pretty ambitious goal. Yet he appears to be well on his way to reaching it. Tim was sworn in to the US Senate in 2013, the first African American senator from the South since Reconstruction.[7]

It all started with a sandwich and a fellow who was willing to walk across the street and offer some encouragement. Maybe we could do something similar?

Look the Simon Peters of your world in the eye, and call forth the Rocky within them by . . .

Listening intently. A desperate woman once came to see Jesus. She was out of doctors, money, and hope. But worst of all she was out of friends. Her sickness rendered her ceremonially unclean, cut off from her family and any house of worship. For more than a decade she'd been ostracized from people. Then Jesus came to town. He was on his way to treat the daughter of the synagogue leader. The crowd was thick, and people were pushing, but she was desperate. Threading her arm through the crowd, she reached the hem of his garment. And when she touched the hem of him, the bleeding stopped. "'Who touched me?' Jesus asked" (Luke 8:45 NIV). The woman shrank back. A dozen years of rejections had made her wary of attention. But Jesus said again that someone had touched him. And this time she spoke up. "She came shaking with fear and knelt down in front of Jesus. Then she told him the whole story" (Mark 5:33 CEV).

The whole story! How long had it been since someone had listened to her story? Jesus took time to hear her speak. He had reason not to do so. The crowd was waiting, the city leaders were standing, a girl was dying, people were pressing, the disciples were questioning, but Jesus? He was listening. He stopped what he was doing, and he listened. He didn't have to. Healing the affliction would have been enough. Enough for her. Enough for the crowds. But not enough for Jesus. He wanted to do more than heal her body. He wanted to hear her story. The miracle restored her health. The listening restored her dignity. And what he did next, the woman never forgot. He affirmed her. He called her "daughter." This is the only time in the Gospels that he called a woman by that name. "Daughter, be of good cheer; your faith has made you well. Go in peace" (Luke 8:48).

Do this for someone. Ask someone to tell you his—or her—story. Resist the urge to interrupt or correct. Turn off the television. Log off from the internet. Close your laptop; silence your cell phone. Give the rarest of gifts: your full attention.

Praising abundantly. Biblical encouragement is no casual, kind word but rather a premeditated resolve to lift the spirit of another person. "Let us consider how we may spur one another on toward love and good deeds" (Heb. 10:24 NIV). The verb *consider* means "to perceive clearly . . . understand fully, consider closely."[8]

John Trent recalls a story about a young father whose daughter was going through the "terrible twos." She was cute but strong-willed and almost more than he and his wife could handle. The father decided to take the child out for breakfast and tell her how much they valued and loved her. Over pancakes he told her, "Jenny, I want you to know how much I love you, and how special you are to Mom and me. We prayed for you for years, and now that you're here and growing up to be such a wonderful girl, we couldn't be more proud of you."

When he finished, his daughter said, "Longer, Daddy, . . . longer." The father continued to affirm and encourage her. Once again when he attempted to stop, she pleaded for him to keep going. She did so two more times. "This father never did get much to eat that morning, but his daughter got the emotional nourishment she needed so much. In fact, a few days later, she spontaneously ran up to her mother and said, 'I'm a really special daughter, Mommy. Daddy told me so.'"[9]

Do you know someone who needs unbridled encouragement? Of course you do. Everyone needs a cheerleader. So be one. "Look for the best in each other, and always do your best to bring it out" (1 Thess. 5:15 THE MESSAGE).

In the mid-1930s a YMCA instructor pitched an idea for a class to his supervisor. It was based on some principles he had learned while working as a salesman in Warrensburg, Missouri. The directors couldn't afford to pay him the regular two-dollar-a-night fee, so he agreed to teach it on a commission basis.

Within a couple of years the course was so popular the instructor was earning thirty dollars a night instead of two. A publishing executive heard the messages and encouraged the instructor to compile them in a book. Dale Carnegie did. His book *How to Win Friends and Influence People* stayed on the *New York Times* bestseller list for a decade. What is the message of the book? Arguably it can be reduced to one phrase: "Encourage one another." The chapter "The Big Secret of Dealing with People" urges readers to "be hearty in your approbation and lavish in your praise."[10]

Here is an idea. Call a friend or relative, and begin the conversation with these words: "Can I have 120 seconds to tell you what a great person you are?" Then let it loose. Build him up. Affirm her. Embarrass him. Drench her in words of encouragement. Imitate the apostle Paul, who told his friends in Ephesus, "I didn't skimp or trim in any way. Every truth and encouragement that could have made a difference to you, you got" (Acts 20:20 THE MESSAGE).

Years ago I became friends with a preacher in Houston. After a wonderful meal together he asked me, "Do you do text messages?" (I'm old enough for him not to make assumptions.) I told him I did, so we swapped phone numbers. A few days later I received a text from him saying, "I am changing your name. You are no longer Max. You are Mighty Max!"

You might think I'd shrug off such a title. I'm a sixty-four-year-old minister. I operate in the formal world of pulpits and Bible study. Mighty Max? That's the stuff of elementary school playgrounds, right?

Not to me it isn't. When I see his name on my phone, I hurry to open the text. I love to be encouraged. We all do. So let's make happiness happen. Let's encourage one another.

Call someone "mighty." Call someone "special." Call someone "Rocky."

Call forth the Peter from within a Simon.

Give the gift that God loves to give: the gift of encouragement.

3

Don't Pet the Peeves

Be patient, bearing with
one another in love.

—Ephesians 4:2 NIV

He picks his teeth in public.

She has this odd manner of clearing her voice every few moments.

He can't watch the news without spouting his opinions.

She must apply her makeup with a putty knife.

He cuts off cars in traffic.

She cuts off people in conversations.

He's as edgy as a porcupine.

She is too laid back and soft spoken.

He rubs you the wrong way.

She gets on your nerves.

Irritating. Aggravating. Exasperating. Infuriating.

Grrr.

If only people would stop behaving like people. If only people would wear deodorant, use mouthwash, close their mouths when they chew, quiet their screaming babies, and clean up their trashy lawns.

There is a way the world should run. And when others behave in ways we don't like, we call that a pet peeve. Not a colossal divide or hostile rivalry or legal violation. Just a pet peeve. A pet (smallish, personal, individual) peeve (quirk, peculiarity). A pet peeve.

———

One of my pet peeves was tested the other night when Denalyn and I went to a movie, a very funny movie at a very full theater. There were hardly any seats left. We finally found two empty chairs on the aisle in the next to last row.

Did I mention that the movie was funny? I thought it was. So did the fellow behind me. But he brought a new dimension to movie enjoyment. Whereas everyone else laughed after the comicality, he laughed prior to it. As he saw the humor coming, he began to chuckle, kind of a chesty "heh-heh-heh." Then he began to prep his wife and, in doing so, prepped us all. "He's gonna fall. Watch, honey. He's gonna fall. He doesn't see the curb. He's gonna fall." Then came the big moment and his announcement: "I told you! He fell! He fell!" Then he would break into wall-shaking laughter that buried the next few lines. Peculiar behavior.

What pets your peeve?

I know a woman who has a pet peeve about facial hair. Must be something Freudian, although Freud had a beard. For whatever reason she does not like beards. When I grew a beard, she expressed her displeasure. More than once. My facial follicles left her harried. On several occasions she waited in the reception line after the worship service and expressed her opinion. Each time I wondered, *Is my beard worth this frustration?*

Joy is such a precious commodity. Why squander it on a quibble?

The phrases we use regarding our pet peeves reveal the person who actually suffers. He "gets under my skin" or "gets on my nerves," or she is such a "pain in my neck." Whose skin, nerves, and neck? Ours! Who suffers? We do! Every pet peeve writes a check on our joy account.

Suppose a basket of Ping-Pong balls represents your daily quota of happiness. Each aggravation, if you allow it, can snatch a ball out of your basket.

- He left his dirty clothes on the floor. A joy ball vanishes.
- She waits until the last minute to apply her makeup. Plop! There goes another one.
- I don't know why people get tattoos.
- I don't know why my tattoo is his business.
- Big trucks shouldn't take up two parking places!
- Preachers shouldn't grow facial hair!

There go the joy balls, one by one, until the joy is gone.

How can you help people smile if you have a hole in your happiness basket? You can't. For this reason the apostle Paul said, "Be patient, bearing with one another in love" (Eph. 4:2 NIV).

The apostle's word for *patient* is a term that combines "long" and "tempered."[1] The short-tempered person has a hair-trigger reaction. The patient person is "long tempered." The word *tempered* literally means "taking a long time to boil."[2] In other words not quickly overheated. Irks come with life, but they need not diminish life.

The patient person sees all the peculiarities of the world. But rather than react, he bears with them. Thanks for the realism, Paul. There are many times when we enjoy one another, delight in one another, and even relish one another. Yet there are occasions when it takes a Herculean act of forbearance just to put up with one another. Paul's verb means exactly that: to tolerate, endure, and forbear. Other translations bring this to light:

"Be patient . . . , making allowance for each other's faults" (NLT).
"Accept life with humility and patience, making allowances for each other" (PHILLIPS).
"Tolerate one another" (THE VOICE).

Denalyn's thirty-seven years of marriage to me, the king of quirks, qualifies her for a PhD in this subject.

> When I drive, my mind tends to wander. When it does, the car slows to a crawl. (*"Max, pay attention."*)
>
> I repair things at risk of ruining them. (*"Max, I told you I could call a handyman."*)
>
> I change bedrooms in the middle of the night. I have no explanation or justification. I just wake up in need of new pastures. (*"Max, where did you end up last night?"*)
>
> My jaw makes a popping noise when I eat steak. (*"Max, you're distracting the people at the next table."*)
>
> I'm good for thirty minutes at a party. She's good for two hours. (*"Max, we just got here."*)
>
> Sending me to the grocery store is like sending me to the Amazon. I may never emerge. (*"You've been gone for two hours, and you only bought potato chips?"*)

Yet Denalyn is the happiest person within a dozen zip codes. Ask her friends or ask my daughters. They will tell you she's married to an odd duck, but she has the joy level of a kid at a carnival. Here is her secret: She's learned to enjoy my idiosyncrasies. She thinks I'm entertaining. Who would've thought? In her eyes I'm a candidate for an oddball Oscar.

To be clear, she lets her opinions be heard. I know when I've tested her patience. Yet I never fear failing the test and am happier for it.

Happiness is less an emotion and more a decision, a decision to bear with one another.

By the way, don't people bear with you? The next time you find it difficult to live with others, imagine what it is like to live with you.

Or, to use the lingo of Jesus, don't obsess about the speck of dust in another person's eye while ignoring the beam in your own eye. Anyone who thinks Jesus never cracked a joke hasn't read these words from the Sermon on the Mount:

> Why do you notice the little piece of dust in your friend's eye, but you don't notice the big piece of wood in your own eye? How can you say to your friend, "Let me take that little piece of dust out of your eye"? Look at yourself! You still have that big piece of wood in your own eye. You hypocrite! First, take the wood out of your own eye. Then you will see clearly to take the dust out of your friend's eye. (Matt. 7:3–5 NCV)

Jesus envisioned a fellow who has a two-by-four sticking out of his eye. It protrudes like Pinocchio's nose. Every time he turns around, people duck for cover. His wife refuses to sleep with him for fear that he'll roll over and knock her out. He can't play a round of golf. Every time he looks down at the ball, his stick sticks into the ground.

But even though the beam is in his eye, it's never on his mind. He's naive regarding the stares of others. When they stare, he assumes they like his shirt. He doesn't see the log in his own eye but can't help but notice a man who stands across the street dabbing his eye with a tissue. With great aplomb the fellow with the extended redwood looks to the right and the left, causing people in both directions to scatter, and then marches across the avenue and declares, "You ought to be more careful. Don't you know that if you get something in your eye, it can be harmful?" Then he smugly turns and struts down the street.

Bizarre? You bet. On target? Yes, sirree, Bob. We have eagle-eye vision when it comes to others but can be blind as moles when we examine ourselves. Were we to be honest, brutally honest, don't we spend more time trying to fix others than we should? Don't we have more expertise on the faults of our friends than the faults of ourselves?

We tend to be like the fellow on the interstate. As he was driving, he received a call from his wife. She was panicked. "Honey, be careful. I just heard on the radio that some fellow is traveling down the highway on the wrong side of the road!"

The husband's reply was equally urgent. "That's not the half of it, sweetheart. It's not just one car going the wrong way. It's hundreds!"

You think the world needs more tolerance? Then be tolerant. You wish people would quit complaining? When you quit, the world is minus one whiner. Nobody gives a hoot about the poor? The hoot level will increase with your compassion. If you want to change the world, begin with yourself. Before you point out the specks in the eyes of others, make sure you aren't sporting a sequoia limb.

D. L. Moody was one of the most influential Christians of his generation. He led thousands of people to faith and established many institutions of education and training. Despite his success he had a reputation for being a humble man, unimpressed with himself and gracious toward others. He was famous for saying, "Right now I'm having so much trouble with D. L. Moody that I don't have time to find fault with the other fellow."[3]

Jesus' teaching did not preclude the place of constructive criticism. He simply urged us to follow the proper sequence. "*First*, take the wood out of your own eye. Then you will see clearly to take the dust out of your friend's eye" (Matt. 7:5 NCV, emphasis mine).

There is a time to speak up. Before you do, check your motives. The goal is to help, never to hurt. Look at yourself before you look down on others. Rather than put them in their place, put yourself in their place.

The truth is we all drop the ball on occasion. I could relate to the mistake of the ninety-year-old woman named Marie who decided that Christmas shopping was simply too difficult for someone her age. She chose to send checks to family and friends. On each card she wrote, "Buy your own present."

She enjoyed the flurry of holiday activities. Not until after Christmas did she get around to cleaning off her desk. Imagine her chagrin when she found under a stack of papers the checks she had forgotten to include.[4]

I could have done the same thing.

Don't we owe it to one another to bear with one another?

During the celebration of his thirtieth wedding anniversary, a friend of mine shared the secret of their happy marriage. "Early on, my wife suggested an arrangement. She would make all the small decisions and would come to me for all the major ones. Wouldn't you know that all these years have passed, and we haven't had one major decision."

Facetious, for sure. Yet there is wisdom in acknowledging the relatively small number of major decisions in life. The clear majority of details in the world are simply that—details. Small stuff. Don't sweat the small stuff, and you won't sweat much at all.

During the next few days you'll be tested. A driver will forget to turn on his blinker. A passenger on the airplane will talk too loudly. A shopper will have fifteen items in the "ten items or less" checkout line. Your husband is going to blow his nose like a foghorn. Your wife is going to take her half of the garage in the middle. When they do, think about your Ping-Pong ball basket.

Don't give up a single ball. No pet peeve is worth your joy or theirs.

Remember the fellow who sat behind me at the movies? With the words you just read fresh on my mind, I decided to practice what I preach. And rather than get mad at him, I began to laugh with him. I laughed at his advance-warning laughter. I laughed when he told his wife what was coming. I laughed when he laughed. Then I laughed at the fact that he laughed. It occurred to me that I was getting entertained from both sides. The screen in front and the fellow in back! Comedy in stereo. It was like a double feature at the same time!

Patience has a boomerang effect. As we bear with one another, we preserve our joy and discover new reasons to smile.

Easy to do? No.

But essential? Absolutely. Life is too precious and brief to be spent in a huff.

One of my favorite places on earth is a grove that sits on the Guadalupe River only minutes from my house. It's a peaceful place. Lazy, puffy clouds float overhead. A tall bluff barricades the strong winds. Bass swim among the rocks. Grass grows along the bank. And trees, oh the trees. Cypresses line the river's edge. Mesquite and Texas live oaks cluster in the draw. They stretch out their limbs and dig their roots into the soil-covered caliche. They weather the winters and celebrate the summers.

And they are all bent. There's not a straight trunk among them. They lean and turn. There is no perfect tree. Even so, they provide the perfect place to find peace. Fishermen doze in their shade. Birds build nests on their branches. Squirrels quarry homes from their trunks.

Humanity is like that grove of trees. Though we attempt to stand tall, none of us succeed. We twist and turn and have our gnarly bark. Some of our trunks are mossy. Some of our branches are heavy. We are a collection of bent timber. And that's okay.

There is beauty in our bentness.

So enjoy the Society of the Bent Timber. Cut people some slack.

Ease up. Reduce your number of peeves, and be patient with the people who pet them.

The world, for all its quirky people, is a wonderful place to live.

The sooner we can find the beauty, the happier we will be.

4

The Sweet Sound of a Second Fiddle

Regard one another as
more important.

—PHILIPPIANS 2:3 NASB

It was a big day in the Lucado house when we purchased a piano. Denalyn loves to play music, and we wanted our daughters to share her passion.

Jenna was five years old. Andrea was three. Sara was a newborn. They were too young to accomplish much on the keyboard but not too young to put on a recital for Daddy. So they did. Almost nightly. Perhaps it was a ploy to postpone bedtime. If so, it worked. What father can resist this invitation: "Daddy, can I play you a song?"

"Me too, Daddy. Can I play you something on the piano?"

"Of course," I'd say. Consequently the scene repeated itself often. Little girl on piano bench. Clad in footie pajamas. Hair still wet from the bath. Pounding the keys more than playing them. Upon completion she would bounce down from the bench and curtsy. I would applaud. Denalyn would applaud. Sister number two would take her turn; the scene would be repeated. It was a delight . . . most nights . . . except for the fights. (Sorry, Jenna and Andrea, but there were a few.)

Jenna would, in Andrea's opinion, play too long. Andrea would climb up next to Jenna and start edging her off the bench. Or Andrea would mess up the song, and Jenna would insist on showing her how to play correctly. Andrea didn't want help. A squabble would ensue.

"But, Daddy, she's not playing it right."

"But, Daddy, it's my turn."

"But, Daddy . . ."

What they didn't understand and what I would try to explain was this: Daddy wasn't grading the song. Daddy didn't need to be impressed. Daddy didn't need a performance, a presentation, or a contest. Daddy just enjoyed being with his girls. Competition and comparison turned my little darlings into tyrants. "Can't we just be together?" I'd say.

Jesus once said the same to two sisters. In their house competition and comparison threatened to ruin a good evening.

As Jesus and the disciples continued on their way to Jerusalem, they came to a certain village where a woman named Martha welcomed him into her home. Her sister, Mary, sat at the Lord's feet, listening to what he taught. But Martha was distracted by the big dinner she was preparing. She came to Jesus and said, "Lord, doesn't it seem unfair to you that my sister just sits here while I do all the work? Tell her to come and help me."

But the Lord said to her, "My dear Martha, you are worried and upset over all these details! There is only one thing worth being concerned about. Mary has discovered it, and it will not be taken away from her." (Luke 10:38–42 NLT)

Gospel writer Luke embedded in his first sentence a few hints about the personality of Martha. "Martha welcomed [Jesus] into her home" (v. 38 NLT).

Martha was the one-person welcoming committee. Not Martha and Mary. Not Martha and Mary and Lazarus. Just Martha.

In my imagination she stands on the porch and welcomes Jesus into "her home." Not *their* home. Hers. Lazarus lives there. Mary lives there. But this is Martha's domain.

And this is Martha's moment. Wide-open arms. "Come in, come in!" This is a big day. And Martha has in mind a "big dinner" (v. 40 NLT).

She escorts Jesus into the living room and offers him a chair. She gestures to his friends to make themselves at home. Jesus takes a seat, and Martha is about to do the same when she hears a noise from the kitchen.

Ding, ding. The soup is ready. The carrot-ginger soup that her namesake prepared on *The Martha Stewart Show*. Martha of Bethany remembers Martha of Stewart's warning not to let the soup get too hot or sit too long.

"Excuse me, Jesus," she says. "I need to mind the soup."

She hurries into the kitchen, grabs her apron off the hook, and ties it behind her back. She slides the pot off the burner, dips a wooden spoon into the soup, and samples it. She nearly gags. It is as bland as egg whites. That's when she realizes she'd forgotten the ginger! Martha of Stewart had looked at the camera and reminded, "Don't forget the ginger." But what had Martha of Bethany forgotten? The ginger. She throws open the wooden shutters and looks into the adjacent room. The disciples are chatting, laughing, talking.

"Dinner might be late!" she announces.

Jesus looks up and smiles. "No problem."

Martha feverishly sets about making more soup. Skipping the soup course, of course, is out of the question. She is preparing a "big dinner." She has the evening all mapped out in her mind. She will give Jesus soup. The disciples will watch. Yea verily the celestial audience will pause as Jesus will all but fall over with delight. "This soup is delicious," he will say. "Divine! Heavenly! The broth of angels!"

Martha will blush and pretend to dismiss the compliment. "Oh, Jesus, it's nothing. I just threw it together." By now a crowd will have gathered on the front lawn. Perhaps a news truck or two. They will pass the word up and down the street. "Jesus is in Martha's house, and he loves Martha's soup."

Of course, none of that celebration will happen if Martha doesn't make the soup. So she relights the stove.

Then she checks the meatloaf. It has to be basted twice, once with tomato sauce and once with honey. It is time for basting number two. She sets the meatloaf on the counter. As she opens the pantry to fetch the honey, she spots the pitcher of mint tea on the counter. Horror of horrors! "I forgot to serve the mint tea!" What kind of hostess is she? She grabs a tray, fills glasses with ice, and hurries through the swinging doors.

Jesus by now is surely surly with thirst. She expects him to glare at her, glance at his watch, and arch his eyebrows. But he isn't upset. He is sitting on the edge of his chair telling a story. His eyes are dancing. His hands are motioning. The disciples are smiling at his description of a Jewish boy who was feeding pigs.

And right smack in front of him, sitting cross-legged on the floor, is Mary, her baby sister.

"Pigs?" Mary asks.

"Yes, pigs!" Jesus affirms.

Martha steps over with her apology and tray of tea. "I am so sorry. I forgot the tea. You must think I am a terrible hostess. But, you see, I forgot the ginger and had to remake the soup. And the meatloaf . . . oh, the meatloaf!"

She sets the tray on the table and hurries back into the kitchen. She slaps sauce on the meatloaf. "Just in time," she says as she places it back in the oven.

She takes the cutting board and begins slicing veggies. Through the open wooden shutters she sees Mary and Jesus. Her sister is laughing. Jesus is gearing up to tell another story. That's when it dawns on Martha. *Why isn't Mary helping me?* Mary could have cut the carrots or washed the celery. She could certainly do something.

Martha turns up the heat on the soup. And she feels the heat rise in her heart. Did her sister not know there was work to be done? The silverware is still in the drawer. The glasses are still in the pantry.

Martha releases an audible sigh. She carries an armful of plates into the dining room and sets them loudly on the table. No response. She feels her jaw tighten as she returns to the kitchen to stir the soup.

Within moments she marches back into the living room with the wooden spoon still in hand and slaps it in her palm, demanding, "Lord, doesn't it seem unfair to you that my sister just sits here while I do all the work? Tell her to come and help me" (v. 40 NLT).

All conversation stops.

A dozen sets of eyes turn.

Mary looks down.

Jesus looks up.

Martha, cheeks flushed with anger, scowls. Her words hang in the air like the scrape of a fingernail on chalkboard.

What had happened to hospitable Martha, welcoming Martha? Luke gives us the answer. "Martha was distracted by the big dinner she was preparing" (v. 40 NLT). She had *big* plans to make a *big* impression with her *big* event. Instead she made a *big* mess. She became "worried and upset over all these details!" (v. 41 NLT).

Of all the ironies. Martha was in the presence of the Prince of Peace, yet she was the picture of stress.

What happened? What is the lesson behind Martha's meltdown?

That it's a sin to cook? That hospitality is the Devil's tool? No. The Bible makes a big deal out of parties and banquets. That it was wrong for her to expect Mary to help? Of course not.

Martha's downfall was not her work or request; it was her motivation. I can't help but think that she wasn't serving Jesus; she was performing for him. She wasn't making a meal for him; she was making a big deal about her service. She was suckered in with the subtlest of lies: self-promotion.

Self-promotion is all about self: "Look what I've done. Look what I've made."

Self-promotion has little room for others: "She just sits."

Self-promotion even bosses Jesus: "Tell them to get to work!"

Not a pretty sight.

Not a pleasant person.

Tell me, of the two sisters in the story, which would you rather spend time with—Martha or Mary?

The question is relevant. Might there be a Martha among us? Might there be a bit of Martha within us? Does our service for Jesus ever turn us into scowling grumps?

Hannah Whitall Smith, author of *The Christian's Secret of a Holy Life*, was raised in a churchgoing home. Years before coming to Christ she recorded her impression of Christians in her journal.

Some look almost as if they think it is a sin to smile or speak a pleasant word. It appears to me that religion is supposed to make one happy, not miserable and disagreeable. . . .

Instead of a cheerful voice there is a long, drawling, melancholy whisper . . . instead of love and concern for those who have not yet found the path of life. There is a cool standoffishness, a feeling of "I'm

better than you"—that effectually closes off the slightest opening. . . .
Instead of a winning gentleness and loving-kindness to those around
them, there is a kind of hidden snappishness and a continual compar-
ing of oneself with them, followed by a disagreeable dictatorianism.
And so, instead of the noble, beautiful, humble, liberal-minded, and
happy religion I have so often pictured to myself, I see it as cross,
gloomy, proud, bigoted, and narrow-minded.[1]

Perhaps Hannah had met a few Marthas. It's a slippery slope, this
thing of self-promotion. What begins as a desire to serve Christ metas-
tasizes into an act of impressing people. When that happens, gifted
Marthas become miserable mumblers. It's easy to see why. If your happiness depends on the applause and approval of others, you'll yo-yo up
and down, based on the fickle opinion of people. If noticed, you'll strut.
If unnoticed, you'll grumble.

Our generation's fascination with social media has taken addic-
tion to adulation to a whole new level. We measure success in "likes,"
"retweets," "thumbs-up," and "friends." Self-images rise and fall upon the
whim of clicks and Facebook entries. Social media is social comparison
on steroids! Does it make sense to hinge your joy on the unpredictable
reactions and reviews of people you may not even know?

Yet the Martha within is not easily silenced. She showed up in my
heart not long ago. A Christian conference was being held in our city.
One of the keynote speakers canceled at the eleventh hour. I received a
call from the organizers. Could I fill the slot?

May I confess my first thought? *Me fill in for someone else? Me, your
second choice? Your backup plan? Your plan B?* I declined the offer. My
reaction was self-centered and nauseating.

Mark it down. When ministry becomes vain ambition, nothing

good happens. Martha gets snappy. Max gets puffy. And Jesus does not get served. No wonder Paul was so insistent: "Do nothing out of selfish ambition" (Phil. 2:3 NIV).

I am not God's MVP.

You are not God's VIP.

We are not God's gift to humanity. He loves us and indwells us and has great plans for us. God can use each of us, but he doesn't need any of us. We are valuable but not indispensable.

> Can the ax boast greater power than the person who uses it?
>> Is the saw greater than the person who saws?
> Can a rod strike unless a hand moves it?
>> Can a wooden cane walk by itself? (Isa. 10:15 NLT)

We are the ax, the saw, the rod, and the cane. We do nothing apart from the hand of God.

Nothing. "So the one who plants is *not important*, and the one who waters is *not important*. Only God, who makes things grow, is important" (1 Cor. 3:7 NCV, emphasis mine).

What gift are you giving that he did not first give? What truth are you teaching that he didn't first teach? You love. But who loved you first? You serve. But who served the most? What are you doing for God that God could not do alone?

How kind of him to use us.

How wise of us to remember Paul's antidote for joy-sucking self-promotion: "With humility of mind let each of you regard one another as more important than himself" (Phil. 2:3 NASB, 1977).

Jesus surely had a smile on his face when he gave the following instructions:

When someone invites you to dinner, don't take the place of honor. Somebody more important than you might have been invited by the host. Then he'll come and call out in front of everybody, "You're in the wrong place. The place of honor belongs to this man." Red-faced, you'll have to make your way to the very last table, the only place left.

When you're invited to dinner, go and sit at the last place. Then when the host comes he may very well say, "Friend, come up to the front." That will give the dinner guests something to talk about! (Luke 14:8–10 THE MESSAGE)

Happy are the unentitled! Expecting the applause of others is a fool's enterprise! Do yourself a favor and assume nothing. If you go unnoticed, you won't be surprised. If you are noticed, you can celebrate.

Here is a helpful exercise that can turn your focus off yourself and on to others. During the next twenty-four hours make it your aim to celebrate everything good that happens to someone else. Keep a list. Develop your "rejoice with those who rejoice" (Rom. 12:15 NIV) muscle. The instant you see something good done by or for another person, let out a whoop and a holler, silently if not publicly. Throw some confetti. Can you envision the fun you will have?

You won't begrudge the good weather enjoyed by Floridians; you'll celebrate their sun-kissed day. Your colleague's promotion will activate happiness, not resentment. The sight of studious Mary won't create a grumbling Martha. Just the opposite. You will thank God for the attention she gives to spiritual matters.

By the end of the day, I daresay, you will be whistling your way through life.

Make a big deal out of yourself, and brace yourself for a day of disappointments. Make a big deal out of others, and expect a blue-ribbon day. You will move from joy to joy as you regard other people's success as more important than your own.

Three angels once took note of a saintly man. He did so much good for so many people that the angels went to God with this request: "That man deserves a special gift. He is so unselfish. He always helps others. Let's reward him."

"With what?" God asked.

"With the gift of eloquence," one angel suggested.

"With the gift of wisdom," offered the second.

"Or the gift of leadership," opined the third angel.

"Why don't you ask him what he would like?" God suggested.

The angels agreed and approached the man.

"We would like to give you a gift."

The man said nothing.

"Any gift you want," the angels explained.

"Would you like to have the gift of eloquence so you can preach?"

"We can give you wisdom so you can counsel."

"Or we will give you the gift of leadership so you can direct the lives of people."

The man looked at the angels and asked, "I can have any gift?"

"Yes."

"Any gift?"

"Yes."

"Then I know what I want."

"Tell us! It will be yours."

"I want to do good and not know that I did it."

From that day forward wherever the man's shadow passed, good things happened. Plants flourished. People laughed. The sick were healed. Merchants succeeded. And the man, unburdened by the knowledge of his success, smiled.

Blessed is the Christian whose focus is on others.

Miserable is the Christian whose focus is on self.

If your desire to be noticed is making you miserable, you can bet it is doing the same for others. Stop being a Martha. Get back to basics. If you have a song to play on the piano, for heaven's sake play it. But play it to please him. You'll be amazed how peaceful the evening will be.

5

The Fine Art of Saying "Hello"

Greet one another.

—ROMANS 16:16

The boss had all he could take. He'd endured more than any CEO should have to, he decided. He'd had it *up to here*. He'd reached his saturation point. *No more!* he resolved, and he left his staff a two-and-a-half-page letter that began with this paragraph:

> I am taking a leave of absence for a month. . . . I am not sure what I am going to do or where I am going, but I will not be here in the office.

He's not the first executive who felt like turning his back on a mess and walking out. The fact of his frustration was not unique. But what prompted his frustration is worthy of note.

> There has been a history around here of people not respecting each other and as of this moment, it's over. It has gotten to the point where I am afraid to even leave the office for fear that people will begin to air their differences. I have been afraid to take even an extended vacation for myself.
>
> Going forward, people are either going to treat each other with respect, dignity, and courtesy or else I will retire. I have worked too

hard and too long to watch this company be torn down. I'll get out (and cash out) before I allow that to happen.

YOU WILL treat one another respectfully or else I am leaving.

When I return, I will ask several people in the office whether or not they have been treated more respectfully in my absence. If they have, I will roll up my sleeves and get back to work in earnest. If nothing has changed, I will move on.

The frustrated boss went so far as to leave his organization specific assignments to fulfill during his thirty-day hiatus. Among them, "Simply say 'Good morning.' It's not that hard."

It wasn't the economy that depleted his strength. The leader wasn't exhausted from the hours at work or the competition in the marketplace. It was the toxic atmosphere of the office. His company was in the lumber business. Many of his employees interacted with transport units on the local docks. The macho world of longshoremen and boat captains had contaminated the culture of respect he sought to promote.

The boss kept his word. He didn't return to the premises for a month. When he did, the atmosphere was different. Employees were learning the meaning of the word *considerate*. The gruff demeanor of the men had modified into a kinder, more thoughtful style of interaction. His ultimatum had its desired effect.[1]

Perhaps we need an ultimatum on society. Oh, the "rages" that rage through people: road rage, airline passenger rage, cell phone rage, checkout rage, social media rage, sideline rage, parking lot rage, car alarm rage, and even rage from drivers who honk at people on crutches.

Social media takes rage to a new level. The online banter blisters and bruises. Words we might never say to a person's face, we feel safe to post on the internet. Rudeness has reached the point where we can all relate to the sign I saw in a medical lab: "If you are grouchy, rude, impatient, or inconsiderate, there will be a $10 charge just for putting up with you."

Yes, a tariff on tackiness has its appeal. A more practical response might be the one suggested by the apostle Paul: "Greet one another with a holy kiss" (Rom. 16:16).

Paul gave identical instructions to other churches. Twice to the Corinthians: "Give each other a holy kiss when you meet" (1 Cor. 16:20 NCV), and "Greet each other with a holy kiss" (2 Cor. 13:12 NCV). Then to the Thessalonians: "Give each other a holy kiss when you meet" (1 Thess. 5:26 NCV).

Peter flew the friendliness flag as well. "Greet one another with a kiss of love" (1 Peter 5:14).

We tend to overlook these passages. This is especially true of the admonition to the Romans. Paul had just spent fifteen chapters guiding his readers through the Yosemite forest of Christian doctrine: salvation by faith, sanctification, perseverance of the saints, predestination, and election. And then in chapter sixteen he took up the curious and unexpected crusade of kind greetings. In a meadow of oaks and elms, this command feels like a sapling.

Why the big deal? Why should we be careful to greet one another?

Out of respect. Respect is a mindfulness of another person's situation. Respect notices the new kid in class and says, "Hello." Respect pauses at the desk of the receptionist and says, "Good morning." Respect refuses to hurry through the checkout line without a genuine "Good afternoon" for the cashier. Respect removes her headphones and greets the fellow passenger. Respect removes his hat to salute the competitor, and respect attempts to remove any awkwardness by welcoming the newcomer to church.

Simply greeting one another is not that hard. But it makes a significant difference.

British minister J. H. Jowett told the story of a convict from Darlington, England. He had just been released after three years in jail when he happened to pass the mayor on the street. Expecting nothing more than cold ostracism from the public, he didn't know how to respond when the mayor paused, tipped his hat, and said in a cheery tone, "Hallo! I'm glad to see you! How are you?"

The ex-prisoner mumbled a response and went on his way. The city official thought nothing of it until years later the two accidentally met in another city. The mayor didn't remember the man, but the man had never forgotten the mayor. He said, "I want to thank you for what you did for me when I came out of prison."

"What did I do?"

"You spoke a kind word to me, and it changed my life!"[2]

What is small to you may be huge to someone else.

A greeting in its purest sense is a gesture of goodwill. Whether it be a culturally acceptable kiss on the cheek as is common in parts of Europe, a bow as is common in Asia, an *abrazos y besos* as is common in Latin America, or a warm handshake as is common in our Western culture, a greeting is an unselfish act.

The first beneficiary of a greeting is the one who gives it. A bumper sticker needs to be created that reads "Huggers are happier." That was the conclusion of researchers at Pennsylvania State University. Students were divided into two groups: readers and huggers. The huggers were instructed to give or receive a minimum of five hugs per day over the course of four weeks. The readers were told to record the number of hours each day they spent reading in the same month. Unsurprisingly the huggers fared better on the happiness scale than the readers. (Sh, don't tell the kids in the library.) Hugging boosted the joy level of the participants.[3] A similar study linked hugging with a diminished rate of sickness. The more often people hugged, the less likely they were to get sick.[4]

So greet people for your sake.

And greet people for their sake. The ungreeted individual never thinks, *They ignored me because they love me.* Just the opposite. Insecurity is often the unhappy child of silence. (Anyone who has lingered unnoticed and unaddressed at a party knows this sense of loneliness.)

Last evening Denalyn and I joined three other couples for dinner at one of their homes. We've been friends for decades. We've traveled, played, and raised our families together.

As we were dining, the eldest son of the host family stopped by. He's been through a tough stretch, battling depression, struggling through a divorce. We rose to greet him when he entered the room, not because of his recent turmoil, but, well, because he is a dear friend to all of us.

We chatted and laughed at some stories. He told us about the girls who think it's funny that a bachelor has two cats. It was nice, very enjoyable. But memorable? No. At least not to me. Later that evening he sent this text to his mom:

> Thank you again for tonight. . . . I've never felt so much love walking into a room before. . . . It was kinda crazy. . . . It felt spiritual. . . . I just had this feeling like I was being greeted in heaven or something. That was really powerful. . . . It's like I was instantly surrounded by all this unconditional love, and it just brought me a peace like I never felt before. I think that will stay with me forever.

We just never know, do we? We never know when a gesture of kindness will touch a heart. Perhaps that's why Paul urged us to greet *everyone.* He did not say, "Greet the people you like." Or "Greet the people you know." Or "Greet the people you want to know." He said simply, "Greet one another."

Paul modeled his appeal for unprejudiced kindness. In the thirteen verses prior, he did with his pen what he would have loved to do with his hand. He mentally went from person to person and greeted each one with a holy greeting (Rom. 16:3–16). He saluted twenty-six people by name and, in some cases, their families. His list included

- Epaenetus, his first convert in Asia;
- Mary, a hard worker;
- Amplias, Urbanus, Hermes, Philologus, Julia—names common among slaves;[5]
- Aristobulus, believed to have been the brother of Agrippa I and the grandson of Herod the Great;[6]
- Narcissus, the secretary of Emperor Claudius;[7] and
- Rufus, who may have been the son of Simon of Cyrene, the man who carried the cross for Jesus on the road to Golgotha.[8]

Consider the extent of Paul's greetings. From male to female, Asian to Roman, slave to aristocrat. From the first convert in Asia to the son of a gospel hero. Paul left no one out. His example urges us to follow suit. No selective greetings allowed. No picking and choosing. Everybody greets everybody. Pecking orders leave people pecked on and picked over. You and I may carry a canteen of water, but we don't know who is thirsty. For that reason we are called to offer it to everyone.

For many years David Robinson was a member of our congregation. He was, and is, an icon in the city of San Antonio. He stands 7'1" and is muscular and handsome. In his NBA career he won championships, Olympic gold medals, and MVP awards.

He did not attend church to gain attention, but the initial time he entered our sanctuary, he received just that. As he walked down the aisle looking for a place to sit, every head turned to look at him. I almost had to stop my opening remarks.

About the time he stepped into the sanctuary, so did another guest. A homeless man wandered in off the street. He was everything David was not: slight, bedraggled, and apparently poor. From my vantage point in the pulpit, I could not help but notice the contrast. The congregation was thrilled and enthralled by the presence of the all-star. But with only one exception no one greeted the street dweller.

I'll always be grateful for that one exception. An elder in our church, tenderhearted and kind, made it a point to leave his pew and take a seat next to the drifter. I've wondered if the homeless man was a messenger of sorts, even an angel in disguise, sent by God to test our willingness to receive *all* God's children.

Don't dismiss the value of a sincere salutation. Our Master was seldom more practical than when he said, "When you knock on a door, be courteous in your greeting" (Matt. 10:12 THE MESSAGE). Give people a firm handshake. Make eye contact. Be sincere.

At any gathering you will find two types of people: those who arrive with the attitude that says, "I am so glad to see you" and those whose attitude says, "I am so glad you see me." It's not hard to differentiate between the two.

Let people know you really care, and then expect the boomerang effect.

The Sumter County Church Chronology includes more than a hundred entries detailing the transactions, changes, and history of the churches in the area. Under the date of June 1965 is this unadorned report: "announcement of $178,000 donation to Andersonville Methodist Church by New Jersey resident Robert B. Brown, who had been impressed by the congregation's welcome during a one-time visit years earlier."[9]

A congregation's welcome *many years earlier* during a *one-time visit* so impressed Mr. Brown that he sent a gift from New Jersey to Georgia.

Greet one another for your sake. Experience the joy of showing people they matter.

Greet each other for their sake. What is small to you may be huge to them.

Most of all, greet one another for Jesus' sake.

Parents, how do you feel when someone pays attention to your child? When a teacher offers special help or an adult offers individual attention, don't you appreciate the person for loving your child? So does Jesus. He loves people who love his kids.

In fact, he goes as far as to say, "When you love my kids, you are loving me." Remember his words: "I was a stranger and you made me welcome" (Matt. 25:35 JERUSALEM BIBLE).

Were Jesus to enter a room, every eye would turn and every person would stand. We'd wait in line for the chance to hold his hands and touch his feet. No one would miss the opportunity to welcome our Savior.

According to Jesus we have that opportunity every day. The nervous teenager in the back of the class? When you greet him, you greet Jesus. The single parent who works down the hall? As you make her feel welcome, you make Jesus feel the same. The elderly woman at the grocery store? As you open the door for her, you open the door for Christ. "In so far as you did this to one of the least of these brothers of mine, you did it to me" (Matt. 25:40 JERUSALEM BIBLE).

By the way, the greatest greeting in history has yet to be given. And you can be certain that salutation won't be heard over a phone or through an email. The greatest of greetings will be issued by Jesus to you in person. "You did well. You are a good and loyal servant. Because you were loyal with small things, I will let you care for much greater things. Come and share my joy with me" (Matt. 25:23 NCV).

6

The Power Posture

Pray for one another.

—JAMES 5:16 ESV

braham and Sarah weren't expecting company. They certainly weren't expecting a visit from God. But he came their way one afternoon, uninvited, unannounced, and disguised in the form of a man. Two other men, angels incognito, were with him. We aren't told at what point Abraham realized he was in the presence of God, but it must have been early in the encounter. The patriarch rolled out the red carpet. Bread was baked. A calf was slain. A feast was prepared and offered.

Abraham looked at Sarah. The question, if not on their lips, was all over their faces: Why is God here, and what on earth is he up to? After the feast the divine trio walked away from the camp, heading toward Sodom, the home of Lot, Abraham's nephew. Abraham walked with them for a short distance to send them on their way. At a certain point God paused, wondering to himself, "Shall I hide from Abraham what I am doing?" (Gen. 18:17). "No, I will not," he decided. And he told Abraham that "the outcry against Sodom and Gomorrah is great, and because their sin is very grave, I will go down now and see" (Gen. 18:20–21).

Abraham stood stone-statue still. He knew what God would find in Sodom. He knew the stench of the streets and the wickedness of the people. Yet he believed there were some worth saving. He had family in the city. Maybe that is why he did what he did. "Abraham still stood before the LORD" (Gen. 18:22).

Like a lone tree on the prairie, the father of the faith had enough faith in his Father to position himself between the people who needed mercy and the One who could give it. And he spoke on their behalf. "Abraham came near and said, 'Would You also destroy the righteous with the wicked? Suppose there were fifty righteous within the city; would You also destroy the place and not spare it for the fifty righteous that were in it?'" (Gen. 18:23–24).

Gutsy move. He was just a bedouin shepherd. Hair to his shoulders. Bristly beard reaching his chest. Scruffy and wind bent. Missing a tooth or two. Still, he stood there.

Just as you did. That day at the courthouse. That night in the ER. That time when your colleague confided in you. "I've made a mess of things," he admitted. And you did what Abraham did. You placed yourself between the one who needed help and the One who could give it.

You prayed.

For soldiers. For senators. For prodigals and preachers and prodigal preachers. You dropped a coin in the beggar's cup with a prayer. You ran your hand over the head of your child with a prayer. You read the news of yet another war, divorce, or scandal, and you prayed, *God, have mercy.*

You've done what Abraham did. You've stood where Abraham stood. In between them and him. And you've wondered, *Does God listen?*

Abraham's story gives us reason to hope.

He was bold with God. He begged God to spare certain citizens of Sodom and Gomorrah, saying, "Far be it from You to do such a thing as this, to slay the righteous with the wicked, so that the righteous should be as the wicked; far be it from You! Shall not the Judge of all the earth do right?" (Gen. 18:25).

Thus far in human history no one had summoned the chutzpah to ask God to reconsider his plans. Adam and Eve didn't. Cain complained, but he didn't negotiate. Methuselah had a birthday cake with 969 candles, but never, as far as we know, did he beg God to revisit the drawing board. Nor did Noah. The ark builder stayed mum. But Abraham spoke up. In the nearby tent we can hear Sarah gulping and whispering, "Abe, hush. You're gonna get us all killed!" She huddled in the corner. *Thunderbolts any minute now.*

But God didn't nuke Abraham. He listened to him.

God: "Fifty righteous people and the city is safe."

Abraham walked away and then paused and returned. "Perhaps forty-five?"

God, smiling: "All right, forty-five."

Abraham turned and then touched each finger as if counting. "Maybe forty?"

God: "Forty is fine."

The back and forth continued until they finally settled on a number: ten righteous. Abraham went his way. God went his. And we are left to ponder this astonishing thought: God wasn't miffed; he was engaged. He wasn't put off; he was responsive. While Sodom and Gomorrah were destroyed, the nephew of Abraham escaped.

All because Abraham stood before the Lord.

He did what Scripture urges us all to do: "Pray for one another, that you may be healed" (James 5:16).

Someone you know is under attack. Your neighbor is depressed. Your sibling is off track. Your child is facing an uphill challenge. You may not know what to say. You may not have resources to help. But you have this: you have prayer. According to these promises your prayers prompt the response of God in the lives of those you love:

> The earnest prayer of a righteous person has great power and produces wonderful results. (James 5:16 NLT)

> Come near to God, and God will come near to you. (James 4:8 NCV)

> The LORD is close to everyone who prays to him, to all who truly pray to him. (Ps. 145:18 NCV)

When we pray for one another, we enter God's workshop, pick up a hammer, and help him accomplish his purposes.

My dad invited my brother and me to do something similar. The idea was born at our kitchen table. My brother was nine years old, I was six, and my dad was . . . Well, he was old enough to know this: if you want to build a house, start with a set of plans. So armed with a pencil and a notepad, he went to work. He drew the house of his dreams.

He loved to build. He'd already constructed two homes, including the one in which we lived. But he had bigger dreams. Three bedrooms instead of two. Brick instead of wood. Room to park two cars instead of one. A workshop in the backyard. A basketball goal in the driveway and, most of all, a fireplace.

As he worked on the plans, we stood on tiptoe and peered over his shoulder. We peppered him with suggestions. Maybe a big window in the living room or a swing set in the kitchen.

"You boys want to help me?" he asked.

Is the pope Catholic? Does a one-legged duck swim in circles? Do fish get wet? Of course we wanted to help! And so it was that my brother and I pedaled our bikes to the construction project on Alamosa Street every day after school. I could hardly handle the excitement. Elementary school seemed so elementary. Who had time for math and spelling? I needed to load kitchen tiles and pick up stray nails. I wasn't just a kid in grade school. I was a partner with my papa.

Our heavenly Father has invited us to be his partner too.

Dare we accept the invitation? Our prayers unlock the storehouses of heaven. The link between God's goodness and your friends is your prayers. When you pray, when you speak for the ones who need help to the One who can give it, something wonderful happens.

As thrilling evidence consider the case of the centurion and his servant. The soldier asked Jesus to heal the man. When Jesus asked if he should go to the man's house, the officer stopped him. "Only speak a word, and my servant will be healed" (Matt. 8:8).

Jesus was so impressed with the faith of the soldier that he answered the request on the spot. He didn't inquire about the faith of the slave. He didn't ask if the man had confessed his sins or requested the Messiah's help. Jesus healed the slave because the centurion did what Abraham had done: he placed himself between the needy person and the One who could meet the need.

Let's do the same.

We have the opportunity to offer heartfelt prayers for every person we see. We can pray for the attendant at the grocery store, the nurse in the doctor's office, the maintenance staff in the office building. You don't have to tell them of your intercessory prayer. Then again, I'm surprised at the welcome response from people when I say, "I'd like to pray for you. Do you have any particular needs?"

Not surprisingly, when we seek to bless others through prayer, we are blessed. Studies draw causal links between prayer and faith and health and happiness. Dr. Harold G. Koenig of Duke University concluded, based on an exhaustive analysis of more than fifteen hundred reputable medical studies, that "people who are more religious and pray more have better mental and physical health." He went on to say that spiritual people, those who pursue divine assistance, "cope with stress better, they experience greater well-being because they have more hope, they're more optimistic, they experience less depression, less anxiety, and they commit suicide less often."[1]

The act of praying for others has a boomerang effect. It allows us to shift the burden we carry for others to the shoulders of God. He invites us to cast all our cares upon him (1 Peter 5:7). Impossible burdens are made bearable because we pray about them. Don't fret about politicians. Pray for them. Don't grow angry at the condition of the church. Pray for her. Don't let the difficulties of life suck you under. Give them to God before they get to you.

Rather than fretting about the future of your family, pray for them. Rather than assuming you can do nothing to help others, assume the posture of prayer.

At 4:30 a.m. on November 10, 2008, Eben Alexander's brain began to fail him. Pain shot through his body. He dismissed it as a virus he'd been battling for several days. Within a couple of hours he knew it was more. He was in agony and virtually paralyzed. By 9:30 a.m. his body was stiff and spasmic. His eyes rolled back in his head, and he slipped into a coma.

The surprising and difficult diagnosis was a rare form of E. coli bacterial meningitis. No one could explain its origin. No one dared to hope for survival. Fewer than one in ten million adults contract it annually. Of those, more than 90 percent die.

Ironically the man with the failing brain was a brain surgeon. Dr. Alexander's résumé impresses even the most educated scholar. Duke University School of Medicine. Residency at Massachusetts General Hospital and Harvard. A fellowship in cerebrovascular neurosurgery. Fifteen years on the faculty of Harvard Medical School. Countless brain surgeries. Author of more than 150 chapters and articles for medical publications. Presentations at more than two hundred medical conferences worldwide.

Irony number two: Dr. Alexander was not a spiritual man. He would be the first to tell you he was a realist. He used the tools of modern medicine to heal people. No one was more surprised than he at what he saw during the coma. "There was a whooshing sound, and in a flash I went through the opening and found myself in a completely new world." In this place "shimmering beings arced across the sky." He heard "a sound, huge and booming like a glorious chant." He describes an "explosion of light, color, love, and beauty that blew through [him] like a crashing wave. . . . There seemed to be no distance at all between God and myself."

What was happening? Prayer was happening. The doctor may not have been a spiritual man, but his friends and family were. In Lynchburg General Hospital they began to gather. They knew to pray. Individually and as a community. As the days passed, they wondered if their prayers mattered. On Thursday, three days into the coma, the pastor of their church was called, and a final wave of urgent prayers began, and the prayers began to break through.

Eben wrote, "I moved down through great walls of clouds. There was murmuring all around me, but I couldn't understand the words. Then I realized that countless beings were surrounding me, kneeling in arcs that spread into the distance. Looking back on it now, I realize what these half-seen, half-sensed hierarchies of beings, stretching out into the dark above and below, were doing. They were praying for me."[2]

On Sunday morning he awoke from his coma. Prayers brought the doctor back to earth.

Do you have an Eben in your life? A crisis in your world? Are you called to give hope where hope can't be found? Is prayer all that you have? That's okay. Prayer is all you need.

Besides, nothing activates happiness like intercessory ministry. Try it. Next time you walk through a crowded airport, lift up your heart to heaven and pray something like this: *Lord, bless that man in the gray suit. He appears to be frazzled. And give strength to the mom and the infant. Look with mercy upon those military personnel.* Before you know it, a humdrum hike becomes a significant stroll of faith.

You will feel the same energy my brother and I felt as we helped Dad build the house! Your Father will hear you. After all . . .

You are his child. "Behold what manner of love the Father has bestowed on us, that we should be called children of God!" (1 John 3:1). You are part of his family. You come, not as a stranger but as an heir to the promise. You approach God's throne, not as an interloper but as a child in whom the Spirit of God dwells. You are his!

You are his ambassador. "Now then, we are ambassadors for Christ, as though God were pleading through us: we implore you on Christ's behalf, be reconciled to God" (2 Cor. 5:20). The ambassador represents the king. He speaks with the authority of the throne. He carries with him the imprimatur of the one who sent him. If the ambassador sends a request to the king, will the king listen? If we, God's ambassadors in this world, come to our King with a request, will he listen? By all means.

You are a member of his priesthood. Peter said, "But you are a chosen generation, a royal priesthood, a holy nation, His own special people" (1 Peter 2:9). Although God has no need of our assistance, he invites us to bring it. My father needed no help with the house. Still he welcomed my brother and me to work with him. Why? I can think of only one answer. He loved us. He wanted to pass on to his children his skill and values.

God is doing the same today! Christ himself prays (Heb. 7:25). And he invites us to pray with him. "You also, as living stones, are being built up a spiritual house, a holy priesthood, to offer up spiritual sacrifices acceptable to God through Jesus Christ" (1 Peter 2:5). The job of the Old Testament priest was to intercede for his people before God. So in our intercession we function as priests, standing in the gap between the people of earth and God.

You actually have a "seat with [Christ] in the heavens" (Eph. 2:6 NCV). You speak on behalf of your family, neighborhood, or softball team. Your sphere of influence is your region. As you grow in faith, your district expands. God burdens you with a concern for orphans, distant lands, or needy people. Respond to these promptings by prayer.

Be the Abraham in your cul-de-sac, the centurion in your workforce. Plead with God on their behalf.

Why would he tell us to pray "Thy kingdom come" (Matt. 6:10 KJV) if we have no impact on the coming of the kingdom? God will not turn you away! Your persistent prayers will open God's door for your friends.

My friends Dan and Nancy Pratt tell a prayer story that is worth recounting. They celebrated their fortieth wedding anniversary with a trip they had discussed since the night they got married: a vacation in Hawaii. But anxious moments leading up to the departure almost derailed the excursion.

Dan and Nancy have a thirty-four-year-old son named Bill. A developmentally delayed nonreader, Bill excels in sacking groceries at a nearby grocery store. He greets every person he sees with a high-decibel "Hello!"

Everyone knows Bill.

Bill, however, tends to get lost. Outside of his normal routine, Bill, according to his dad, has a PhD in slip sliding away. The plan was for Bill to fly from San Antonio to Atlanta and spend the week with his brother.

But Mom and Dad began to grow anxious. They talked Bill through the travel process on their daily walks, when they ate, and when they got up in the morning and went to bed at night. Bill seemed to understand the plan. Still, they worried.

So Dan and Nancy turned their worries into prayer. They recruited friends and family to provide prayer protection for Bill along the way. They prayed right up to the time to go to the airport.

Dan acquired a special pass to walk Bill to the gate. Bill was nervous, so they walked up and down the concourse to burn energy. Nancy called twice. The brother in Atlanta called once. The entire family was wound up.

Finally, ten minutes before boarding, Dan walked Bill to the gate. As he handed Bill his boarding pass, two women cried out, "Hey, Bill!" They knew Bill from the grocery store. They were on the same flight. About the time they finished saying hello, a man shouted, "Hey, Bill! Who is going to help me carry out my steaks?" He was en route to Atlanta as well. During the next ten minutes six other people recognized Bill and said hello. By the time he boarded, he had nine friends on the plane to watch out for him, one of whom volunteered to escort him to the care of his brother.

When Dan reported the news to Nancy, her voice broke with emotion. She remembered the assurance from a friend: "Don't worry, Nancy. Ol' Bill will see someone who knows him, and they will take care of him."[3]

Yeah, but nine people?

God heard the prayers of the family and friends.

He will hear yours as well, my friend.

We can do much after we pray, but we can do nothing until we pray. Before we serve, before we teach, before we encourage, we pray. Our calling is to be an Abraham on behalf of the people in our world. Place yourself between them and God, and speak up. Be assured, he will listen.

7

It's Your Serve

Through love serve one another.

—GALATIANS 5:13

I remember him as a large man, built like a concrete block. He wore a crew cut, neckties, and short-sleeved white shirts with an ever-present pocket protector. I was one of four fourth-grade boys who attended his Bible study each Wednesday at the Parkview Church of Christ in Odessa, Texas. The classroom held at least a dozen desks. I do not remember the teacher's name. Nor do I recall any details about his life. Was he a plumber or a postman? I have no idea.

What I recall with startling detail is the evening of February 10, 1965. He attempted to teach his handful of ten-year-old boys the meaning of the seventh chapter of Romans. That is the section in which the apostle Paul confessed the civil war that raged within his heart. The topic was a heavy one for a covey of kids. When he talked about a troubled conscience and the need for forgiveness, I took note.

I gave the teacher no reason to think the class had made an impression on me. I didn't ask any questions or thank him for his words. He likely went home with little or no understanding of the impact of the lesson. If his wife had asked him, "How was your class?" he would have shrugged and said, "I dunno. Those kids don't talk much." What he didn't know is that the freckle-faced redhead on the second row was listening.

———

That night I stepped into my father's bedroom and asked him about heaven. Dad took a seat on the edge of the bed and invited me to join him. He told me about grace. I asked Jesus to forgive me. The following Sunday I was baptized. A new me began.

Over the years I've often thought about that teacher. He wasn't a pastor. He wasn't dynamic. He was prone to fumble over his words. He didn't have a title, seminary degree, or reserved parking place. He never filled a stadium. As far as I know, he never planted a church. He wasn't an expert on church growth or how to solve world hunger. If he left a sizable donation to a nonprofit in his will, I never heard about it. Yet his teaching rerouted my path.

I've not seen him since, but I've seen thousands like him. Quiet servants. The supporting cast of the kingdom of God. They seek to do what is right. They show up. Open doors. Cook dinners. Visit the sick. You seldom see them in front of an audience. That's the last place most of them want to be. They don't stand behind a pulpit; they make sure the pulpit is there. They don't wear a microphone but make certain it's turned on.

They embody this verse: "For you, brethren, have been called to liberty; only do not use liberty as an opportunity for the flesh, but through love serve one another" (Gal. 5:13). These words appear toward the end of a document on liberation. For five chapters the apostle Paul proclaimed, "You are free! Free from sin. Free from guilt. Free from rules. Free from regulations. The yoke of slavery is off, and the liberation has begun."

Our freedom, however, is not an excuse for us to do whatever we want. Just the opposite. Because we are free, we can serve. We voluntarily indenture ourselves to others. In a society that seeks to be served, we seek opportunities to serve others.

Andrew was such a servant. He was the brother of Peter. He came from the same town as James and John. Yet when we discuss the inner circle of Peter, James, and John, we don't mention Andrew. His name never appears at the top of the list of leaders. He lived in the shadow of the others. In the group photo he stood at the side, hands in pockets. Then again, he probably held the camera.

Quiet, however, does not mean complacent. Just because Andrew avoided the limelight, that doesn't mean he lacked fire. He led his brother Peter to Jesus. Peter went on to preach the first sermon. Peter led the Jerusalem church. Peter took the gospel to Gentiles. He wrote epistles that we still read. He defended the apostle Paul. Anyone who appreciates Paul's epistles owes a debt of gratitude to Peter. And anyone who has benefited from the rocklike faith of Peter owes a debt to the servant spirit of Andrew.

And it was the servant spirit of Mary that led God to select her to be the mother of Jesus. She wasn't a scholar or a sophisticated socialite. She was simple. Plain. A peasant. She blended into the crowd. She hailed from Nazareth, a dusty village in an oppressed district in Galilee.

In the social strata of her day, Mary occupied the lowest step. As a Jew she answered to the Romans. As a female she was subservient to males. As a young girl she was second to older women. She was poor, so she was beneath the upper class.

Mary was extraordinarily ordinary. Yet this virtue set her apart: "I am the servant of the Lord. Let this happen to me as you say!" (Luke 1:38 NCV).

When God wants to bring Christ into the world, he looks for servants. No diploma required. No bloodline specified. Bank accounts are not a factor. Place of birth doesn't matter. Let all unassuming people of the world be reminded: God can use you.

Let all proud people of the world be cautioned: God will correct you.

Sin is the word the Bible uses to describe the arrogant streak that causes self-elevation. Sin engenders a sense of entitlement. Sin describes the malady that prompted my snarl in the shopping mall parking lot. A woman snagged my parking place. The parking place I wanted. The parking place I needed. The parking place for which I had been waiting. (I was waiting with my blinker on, for crying out loud!) The parking place I deserved because I was in a hurry, and I am very important, and I do not have time to lollygag at shopping malls, because I am a man of God, and it was the week prior to Christmas.

Holidays are busy times for pastors, and the parking place opened at just the right moment, proof of God's favor upon me. How dare that woman take my blessing! But she did. I thought of saying something to her. I am so glad I held my tongue, because when she saw me drive by, she said, "Hello, Pastor Max! See you Sunday!"

Multiply the arrogance that struck me in the parking lot by seven billion humans who share the same planet. Then multiply it again by the dozens of times it strikes each of us each day. No wonder this world is a mess.

Entitlement certainly struck the mother of James and John.

> Then the mother of Zebedee's sons came to Him [Jesus] with her sons [James and John], kneeling down and asking something from Him.
>
> And He said to her, "What do you wish?"
>
> She said to Him, "Grant that these two sons of mine may sit, one on Your right hand and the other on the left, in Your kingdom." (Matt. 20:20–21)

Sometimes we wonder if the disciples listened when Jesus spoke. Just one page of Scripture prior we read how he told them to imitate the spirit of children (Matt. 19:13–15). He told the rich, young ruler to quit trusting self and start trusting God (Matt. 19:16–21). He declared, "The last will be first, and the first will be last" (Matt. 20:16 NIV). For the third time he predicted his own death, burial, and resurrection (Matt. 20:17–19).

But did any of Jesus' followers ask him to explain the meaning of humility? Did anyone comfort him? No. The only response came from the mother of James and John as she requested cabinet positions for her sons in the new kingdom.

It wasn't enough for her that her sons witnessed the miracles of Christ. It wasn't enough for them to be chosen as apostles, to be designated as members of the inner circle and stand on the Mount of Transfiguration. She wanted their faces to be carved onto the stone of Mount Rushmore with Jesus'. One on his right, the other on his left.

Jesus quickly corrected her desire.

It shall not be so among you; but whoever desires to become great among you, let him be your servant. And whoever desires to be first among you, let him be your slave—just as the Son of Man did not come to be served, but to serve, and to give His life a ransom for many. (Matt. 20:26–28)

Jesus came to serve.

In one of his appearances to his followers, they were on the Sea of Galilee when they heard him call out from the shore. When he told them where to find fish, they realized it was Jesus. Peter plunged into the water and swam to shore. The other disciples grabbed their oars and paddled. When they reached the beach, they saw the most extraordinary sight. Jesus was cooking! He told them, "Come and eat breakfast" (John 21:12).

Shouldn't the roles be reversed? Jesus had just ripped the gates of hell off their hinges. He'd disemboweled the Devil. He'd made a deposit of grace that forever offsets our debt of sin. He'd sentenced the demons to death row and set free every sinner since Adam. He, the unrivaled Commander of the Universe, wore the apron?

Even more, he has yet to remove it. He promises a feast in heaven at which "he will gird himself and have them sit down to eat, and will come and serve them" (Luke 12:37).

Can you imagine the sight? Row after row of food-laden tables. The redeemed of the ages celebrating and singing, and someone asks, "Has anyone seen Jesus?"

"Yes," another replies. "He's on the other side of the banquet room serving ice tea."

> Christ himself was like God in everything.
> But he did not think that being equal with God was something to be used for his own benefit.
> But he gave up his place with God and made himself nothing.
> He was born as a man
> and became like a servant. (Phil. 2:6–7 NCV)

He was content with the humblest of titles. He was content to be called a servant.

Suppose you took that role. Be the family member who offers to wash the dishes after dinner. Be the colleague who serves the staff by arriving on time for each meeting and listening attentively. Be the church member who supports the pastor with prayer and notes of encouragement. Be the neighbor who mows the grass of the elderly couple.

Can you imagine the joy-giving benefits of these decisions?

Of course you can! You've experienced it. When you took a pie to the sick coworker or sang a song to the sick child, were not both of you encouraged because of it? You've been unScrooged from stinginess enough times to know the easiest way to make yourself smile is to make someone else smile first.

Contrast the situation of Moe and Joe. Moe expects everyone to serve him. The moment he awakens he thinks, *Is someone going to bring me coffee?* He leaves the house thinking, *The traffic better be light.* If the service of the convenience store clerk is slow, Moe is mad. If the parking lot attendant forgets Moe's name, Moe grumbles. If the employees at work need more time than Moe wants to give them, Moe lets them know.

Moe has high expectations of the world. He expects to be served. He expects people to cater to his plans, meet his needs, and reward him. Consequently, Moe is seldom happy. The service is too slow, the commute takes too long, and the employees don't remember his name quickly enough.

Moe, miserable Moe.

Joe, on the other hand, measures the success of his day with this standard: Whom can I help today? Since there are always people who need help, Joe is insanely successful. He serves his wife by bringing her coffee in the morning. He serves the convenience store clerk by giving him a smile. He serves the parking lot attendant with an encouraging word. He keeps a positive attitude at work.

Bad weather? Snarly traffic? No problem. The world doesn't exist to take care of him. He exists to take care of others. Circumstances do not affect him. Joe goes to bed with a smile on his face.

Moe is unhappy and makes people frown.

Joe is happy and makes people smile.

Which one are you? Moe? Joe? Or a little of both, Mo-Jo?

Maybe it's time to look at life differently. Make your happiness dependent on how others serve you, and you will always be disappointed. Find happiness in serving others, and . . . Well, you can complete the sentence.

The studies are clear. Doing good does the doer good. A 2010 study of more than forty-five hundred American adults revealed that of the people who volunteered an average of more than one hundred hours per year, 68 percent reported feeling physically healthier. And 73 percent said that volunteerism "lowered my stress levels," and 89 percent stated that service "has improved my sense of well-being."[1] We elevate our joy by giving joy to others.

In a separate study psychologist Bernard Rimland asked participants to list ten acquaintances and characterize them as happy or unhappy. He then asked the participants to review the list and categorize each person as selfish or unselfish. His findings led him to draw a conclusion that echoes the theme of this book: "everyone who was labeled happy was also labeled unselfish."[2] It is in your best interest to look out for the interest of others!

Long before a research team pondered the benefits of service, God was promising them.

> And if you give yourself to the hungry
> And satisfy the desire of the afflicted,
> Then your light will rise in darkness
> And *your gloom will become like midday.*
> And the LORD will continually guide you,
> And satisfy your desire in scorched places,
> And give strength to your bones;

And you will be like a watered garden,

And like a spring of water whose waters do not fail.

(ISA. 58:10–11 NASB, EMPHASIS MINE)

What would happen if everyone took on the role of a servant? How many marriages would be blessed? If politicians set out to serve their people more than serve themselves, would their country benefit? If churches were populated by sincere servants, how many ten-year-old boys would hear the invitation of a lifetime?

In the hallway of my memory hangs a photograph. It's a picture of two people—a man and a woman, a couple in the seventh decade of life.

The man lies in a hospital bed. But the hospital bed is in the living room, not in a hospital room.

His body, for all practical purposes, is useless. Muscles have been so ravaged by ALS that they're stretched from bone to bone like the taut fabric on the spokes of an umbrella.

He breathes through a hose attached to a hole in the base of his throat. And even though his body is ineffective, his eyes are searching. They scan the room for his partner, a woman whose age is concealed by her youthful vigor. Her hair is gray, but she's vibrant and healthy in contrast to the figure lying in the bed.

She willingly goes about her task of the day: taking care of her husband. With unswerving loyalty she does what she's been doing for the past two years. It's not an easy assignment. She must shave him, bathe him, feed him, comb his hair, and brush his teeth.

She holds his hand as they sit and watch television together.

She gets up in the middle of the night and suctions his lungs.

She leans over and kisses his feverish face.

She serves him.

———

She carries on the lineage of Andrew and Mary.

By the time my father took his final breath, the two had been married for more than four decades.

On the day we buried him, I thanked my mom for modeling the spirit of Christ: quiet servanthood.

8

Discomfort Zones

Accept one another, then, just
as Christ accepted you.

—ROMANS 15:7 NIV

O nce upon a time in a land not far from our own, there was a tidy, well-manicured neighborhood. Its residents kept the streets clean, lawns trimmed, and standards high. Each household had two kids, two parents, a dog or cat, and a goldfish. They walked their dogs and waved at the mail carrier and turned out their lights by 10:00 p.m. They enjoyed their quiet lives. But then their tranquility was turned upside down. A man bought the brick house on the corner of Oak and Elm. A single man. Not a family. Not a couple. A single man by the name of Levi.

Levi, as it turned out, drove a Corvette, souped up and top down. Levi, as it turned out, mowed his lawn bare chested. Levi, as it turned out, installed a pool and a deck and a grill and an outdoor sound system. While the rest of the neighbors were winding down for the evening, Levi was cranking it up.

He had parties. His friends came from the seedy side of town. They drove jacked-up pickups and low-riding Chevys. The men wore Dingo boots and tattoos. The women wore tight tank tops. Some men had six-packs for abs; others arrived with six-packs in their hands. They all talked too loud, drank too much, and partied too late into the night.

On Sunday mornings when the fine people of the fine neighborhood drove to church, they looked at the beer cans strewn on the front lawn of the new neighbor and said to their kids, "That man needs Jesus."

And so Jesus came. He walked into the neighborhood and onto the street. He went from house to house asking if anyone had time to talk, play dominoes, or grill burgers.

But who had time for such folly? They had their work and curfews and chores. No one had time for Jesus. No one, that is, except the guy on the corner of Oak and Elm. The guy with the loud car and loud friends. He had time.

Jesus knocked on Levi's door, and Levi invited him in for supper. The two hit it off. They hung out, told jokes, and discussed life. Eventually Levi told Jesus about his sordid past. Jesus told Levi about forgiveness and the future. Levi asked, "Even for me?" Jesus smiled. "Yes, especially for someone like you."

One day Jesus paid him a special visit and gave him this offer: "'Follow me!' So Levi got up, left everything, and followed him" (Luke 5:27–28 ncv).

Levi. Better known as Matthew: Matthew the apostle, the gospel writer, the first-generation follower of Jesus. But before he was Matthew, he was Levi. Before he was stained glass, he was stained merchandise. Before he helped write the Bible, he helped himself to the pockets and purses of his countrymen.

Matthew was a public tax collector, a Jew who worked for the Roman IRS. The emperor allowed tax collectors to collect a duty on anything and everything. As long as Rome got its part, the revenuers could take as much as they wanted. They did. They got rich by making people poor. On their walls was a framed mission statement: "Get all you can and can all you get."

That's how Matthew could afford the Corvette and the parties.

That's why he was brash and wild. He'd long since swapped his dignity and self-respect for a fat wallet and fast car. He was never invited to neighborhood cookouts, never included in the high school reunions. People whispered as he walked past, "That's Levi, the leech." He was a scoundrel, a hustler, slicker than the belly of a snake. He was a tax collector.

Jesus, however, saw potential in Matthew. Matthew saw redemption in Jesus. So when Jesus made the offer, Matthew took it. He joined Jesus' ragtag band of disciples.

But even though Matthew had a new life, he couldn't forget his old friends. He missed the gang. For sure their language was salty and morals were loose. They hung out at gentlemen's clubs and spent weekends at the casinos. They dressed slick, drank too much, and lived too fast, but Matthew had a heart for them. One day he told Jesus, "I like your crew. I like Peter, John, and the others, but I really miss Billy Bob and Bubba Joe and Betty Sue . . ."

Jesus said, "Let me tell you something. To be my friend doesn't mean you can't be their friend. I'd love to meet them."

Matthew perked up. "You would? They aren't the churchgoing type. They aren't welcome in the synagogues."

"No problem. Neither am I. How about throwing a party? We'll get both groups together—Peter and Thomas and Billy Bob and Bubba Sue."

"Actually his name is Bubba Joe. But that's a great idea."

Matthew called the caterer and made a guest list. "Then Levi held a great banquet for Jesus at his house, and a large crowd of tax collectors and others were eating with them" (Luke 5:29 NIV).

This wasn't a simple backyard barbecue. It was a great banquet with a large crowd. Fancy wine. Maître d's. Food on every table, guests in every corner. And not just any guests but a curious confluence of bikers and beauties and Bible toters. The apostles intermingled with the rabble-rousers. It was the happy-hour crowd and the Sunday school class at the same party.

Jesus was thrilled.

The religious leaders, however, were riled.

They were called the Pharisees. Their moniker came from an Aramaic word meaning one who is separate.[1] They were all about separating themselves from sinners. Holiness, by their definition, meant cloisters, quarantines, and isolation. Good people—God's people—circle up their wagons. They don't chum with bad people.

When the Pharisees got wind of the party, they crashed it. They marched into Matthew's house wearing scowls and frowns and holding extra-thick copies of the Bible. They pointed fingers and demanded an explanation from Jesus. "Why do you eat and drink with tax collectors and sinners?" (Luke 5:30 NIV).

Matthew's friends groaned. They knew the drill. They knew they didn't fit in. All their lives they'd been told, "You aren't good enough for God." They began to gather their things so they could leave. The party was over.

"Not so fast," Jesus said in so many words. He stood up—if not literally, at least symbolically. He stood up for Matthew and his friends. "It is not the healthy who need a doctor, but the sick. I have not come to call the righteous, but sinners to repentance" (Luke 5:31–32 NIV).

Jesus peppered the sentence with irony. Pharisees considered themselves spiritually "healthy" and "righteous." In actuality they were unhealthy and self-righteous. But since they did not think they were sick, they saw no need for Jesus.

Matthew and the gang, on the other hand, made room for Jesus. As a result Jesus made room for them.

Do we?

One of the most difficult relationship questions is "What do we do with a Levi?"

Your Levi is the person with whom you fundamentally disagree. You follow different value systems. You embrace different philosophies. You adhere to different codes of behavior, dress, and faith.

You drive a hybrid; he chugs around in a gas-guzzling, air-polluting truck.

You vote red, and she likes donkeys.

You love your husband, and she lives with her wife.

Your Levi is your "opposite you."

"Opposite yous" can drain your joy tank. There is a tension, an awkwardness. Anger—low-grade or high flame—can flare. Inability to manage the relationship can lead to isolation, prejudice, and bigotry.

What if your "opposite you" is your boss? Your next-door neighbor? Your coworker? What if your "opposite you" is your parent or child?

How does God want us to respond to the Levis of the world? Ignore them? Share a meal with them? Leave the room when they enter? Ask them to leave so we can stay? Discuss our differences? Dismiss our differences? Argue? Avoid them?

I wonder if the best answer might be found in this short admonition: "Accept one another, then, just as Christ accepted you, in order to bring praise to God" (Rom. 15:7 NIV).

This passage summarizes a thirty-verse appeal to the Roman church for unity (Rom. 14:1–15:7). Paul began and ended the treatise with the same verb: *accept*. This verb, *proslambanó*, means more than tolerate or coexist. As Anglican priest John Stott wrote, "It means to welcome into one's fellowship and into one's heart. It implies the warmth and kindness of genuine love."[2]

Paul employed the verb when he urged Philemon to welcome the slave Onesimus the same way he would welcome Paul himself (Philem. v. 17). Luke selected it to describe the hospitality of the Maltese to the people who were shipwrecked (Acts 28:2). And, most notably, Jesus used it to describe the manner in which he receives us (John 14:3).

How does he receive us? I know how he treated me.

I was a twenty-year-old troublemaker on a downhill path. Though I'd made a commitment to Christ a decade earlier, you wouldn't have known it by the way I lived. I'd spent five years claiming to be God's child on Sunday mornings and buddying with the Devil on Saturday nights. I was a hypocrite. Two-faced, too fast, and self-centered.

I was lost. Lost as Levi.

When I finally grew weary of sitting in pig slop, I got wind of God's grace. I came to Jesus, and he welcomed me back.

Please note: Jesus didn't accept my behavior. He didn't endorse my brawling and troublemaking. He wasn't keen on my self-indulgence and prejudice. My proclivity to boast, manipulate, and exaggerate? The chauvinistic attitude? All that had to go. Jesus didn't gloss over the self-centered Max I had manufactured. He didn't accept my sinful behavior.

But he accepted *me*, his wayward child. He accepted what he could do with me. He didn't tell me to clean up and then come back. He said, "Come back. I'll clean you up." He was "full of grace and truth" (John 1:14 NIV). Not just grace, but also truth. Not just truth, but also grace.

Grace *and* truth.

Grace told the adulterous woman, "I do not condemn you" (John 8:11 NASB).

Truth told her, "Go and sin no more" (John 8:11).

Grace invited a swindler named Zacchaeus to host Jesus for lunch.
Truth prompted him to sell half of his belongings and give to the
poor (Luke 19:1–8).

Grace washed the feet of the disciples.
Truth told them, "Do as I have done to you" (John 13:15).

Grace invited Peter to climb out of the boat and walk on the sea.
Truth upbraided him for his lack of faith (Matt. 14:28–31).

Grace invited the woman at the well to drink everlasting water.
Truth tactfully reminded her that she had gone through five
husbands and was shacking up with a boyfriend (John 4:4–18).

Jesus was gracious enough to meet Nicodemus at night.

He was truthful enough to tell him, "Unless one is born again, he
cannot see the kingdom of God" (John 3:3).

Jesus shared truth but graciously.

Jesus offered grace but truthfully.

Grace and truth. Acceptance seeks to offer both.

If we offer only grace, then we gloss over the truth. If we offer only
truth, then we dismiss the joy of grace. Our goal is to strike a balance.
Oh, if only the balance were easy to strike. I have tilted in both directions. I have been so zealous for truth that I have forgotten grace. I've
been a crusader for tolerance and omitted truth.

I recall one occasion in which I was attempting to encourage a
woman whose marriage was in shambles. She was considering a divorce.
Her husband was verbally abusive, possibly adulterous. "Go ahead and
leave him," I urged. Several months passed, and I heard nothing from

her. When I finally saw her again, she said, "I am back on my feet, strong in my faith, and it is with no thanks to you."

What?

She said, "You gave me a way out. I needed to be challenged to stay in."

The catchphrase "hate the sin and love the sinner" fits nicely on a bumper sticker, but how do we embed the principle in our hearts?

Maybe these ideas will help.

Reserve judgment. Let every person you meet be a new person in your mind. None of this labeling or preconceived notions. Pigeonholes work for pigeons, not for people.

During the season I was preparing these chapters, I happened to be walking through the downtown area of a major city on a Saturday afternoon. I spotted a haggard-looking man sitting on the concrete steps of a building. He wore a stocking cap, dirty clothes, and a full beard. A can of his favorite beverage sat at his feet.

In some ways the man was a Levi in my world. I might have walked past him. But, well . . . I was in the middle of preaching a series on making happiness happen by living out the "one another" passages, so I set aside my discomfort and sat down beside him. I had taken him for a homeless, unemployed drifter. I was wrong.

Turns out he was gainfully employed as a stagehand. He had just gotten off work from an all-night shift. We talked for a few moments about his career—several decades of setting it up and tearing it down for the best of country music. He told me about some of the singers he had met. He also told me that God had blessed his life and that he felt the favor of the Lord. I'd misjudged him. I walked away a bit embarrassed.

Raleigh Washington is an African American minister who has dedicated much of his life to racial reconciliation. He says that the most important statement in bridge building is this: "Help me understand what it's like to be you."[3]

> Help me understand what it's like to be a teenager in this day and age.
> Help me understand what it's like to be born into affluence.
> Help me understand the challenges you face as an immigrant.
> Help me understand what it's like to be a female in a gray flannel corporation.

Then sit back and listen. Really listen. Listening is a healing balm for raw emotions. (A friend admitted to me, "I often appear to be listening when actually I am reloading.")

"Be in agreement [be like-minded; live in harmony], understanding each other [sympathetic], loving each other as family [showing brotherly love], being kind [tender; compassionate] and humble" (1 Peter 3:8 EXB).

Abraham Lincoln modeled this type of acceptance. During the Civil War when his wife criticized people from the South, he told her, "Don't criticize them, Mary; they are just what we would be under similar circumstances."[4]

We are never ever called to redeem the world. "Savior of humanity" is not on your job description or mine. Encourage, correct, applaud, and admonish? By all means. But save the world? In no way. There is only one Messiah and one throne. He isn't you, and the throne isn't yours.

Resign from the role. To do otherwise is to sentence yourself to a life of misery. The weight of the world will crush you. Recall the party of Levi. Who missed out on the fun? The stern-faced Pharisees.

Happiness happens, not by fixing people but by accepting people and entrusting them into the care of God. Jesus did this. Otherwise, how could he have endured? No one knew humankind's hypocrisy and failings more than he. Christ knew exactly what people needed, yet he gave them time and space to grow. Aren't we wise to do likewise?

Resist the urge to shout. We did a lot of shouting on our elementary school playground. All the boys in Mrs. Amburgy's first-grade class bonded together to express our male superiority. We met daily at recess and, with arms interlocked, marched around the playground shouting, "Boys are better than girls! Boys are better than girls!" Frankly I didn't agree, but I enjoyed the fraternity.

The girls in response formed their own club. They paraded around the school announcing their disdain for boys: "Girls are better than boys." We were a happy campus.

Shouting at Levi feels good. But does it do any good?

It seems to me there is a lot of shouting going on.

On the airwaves, shouting.

On bumper stickers, shouting.

On the news broadcasts, shouting.

On social media, shouting.

All sides shouting.

"We are better than you. We are smarter than you. We are holier than you." Is it possible to have an opinion without having a fit? The apostle Paul was critical of the person who is "full of pride and understands nothing, but is sick with a love for arguing and fighting about words. This brings jealousy, fighting, speaking against others" (1 Tim. 6:4 NCV).

"Do not argue about opinions" (Rom. 14:1 NCV). It is one thing to have an opinion; it's something else to have a fight. When you sense the volume increasing and the heat rising, close your mouth. It's better to keep quiet and keep a friend than to be loud and lose one. Besides, "they are God's servants, not yours. They are responsible to him, not to you. Let him tell them whether they are right or wrong. And God is able to make them do as they should" (Rom. 14:4 TLB).

Let's reason together. Let's work together. And if discussion fails, let love succeed. "Above all things have fervent love among yourselves; for love shall cover the multitude of sins" (1 Peter 4:8 NSRB). If love covers a multitude of sins, can it not cover a multitude of opinions? We need intermezzi of calm in this cacophony of opinions.

Brian Reed served in a military unit in Baghdad, Iraq, in the fall of 2003. He and his unit went on regular street patrols to protect neighborhoods and build peace. It was often a thankless, fruitless assignment. Citizens seemed more interested in receiving a handout than a hand up. Brian said his unit battled low morale daily.

An exception came in the form of a church service his men stumbled upon. The soldiers got out of their military vehicles, intrigued by the sight of a wrought iron nativity: three wise men from the East advertising to all who passed by that this was a Christian gathering in a Christian church.

Brian and his men, armed and armored to the teeth, entered the facility. It was filled with Arabic-speaking Coptic Christians singing and praising God with a worship team and PowerPoint slides. The Americans did not understand a word, but they recognized the image on the screen, a depiction of Jesus. The language was foreign, but the observances were not: fellowship, prayer, the teaching, and the breaking of bread.

When they saw the American soldiers, the Coptic Christians invited them to partake in the Lord's Supper with them. The soldiers removed their helmets and received the sacraments. They then joined the Iraqis on a processional as they made their way out of the sanctuary into a courtyard that ended at the foot of a large wooden cross.

Afterward they smiled, laughed, shook hands, and prayed again.

It was peace in the Middle East.

Brian wrote, "Jesus was there. He showed up in the very place some of us were ready for our air force brethren to blow off the face of the earth. God spoke to me that evening. . . . Celebrating the Lord's Supper and remembering Jesus' sacrifice for our sins was the most important bridge builder and wall destroyer we could have experienced."[5]

"Opposite yous" brought together by the cross of Christ.

In his book *Streams of Mercy,* Mark Rutland refers to a survey in which Americans were asked which words they would most like to hear. He says that he guessed the first answer but never imagined the second and third. Number one: "I love you." Number two: "I forgive you." But the real surprise was number three: "Supper's ready."[6]

Those three phrases summarize the message of Jesus. He came with love, grace, and a dinner invitation. For Matthew and his friends, the dinner happened in ancient Israel. For you, me, and all the other Levis of the world? Heaven's banquet will exceed our fondest dreams.

And we'll be surprised whom we see at the table.

9

Speak Up

Admonish one another.

—COLOSSIANS 3:16 NIV

Your coworker leaves this voice mail: "My father just passed away. I'm on my way to the hospital. I don't know if I can handle this."

Your next-door neighbor explains the appearance of the moving van that sits in front of her house. "My husband is moving out. Says he's done with our marriage."

Your sibling calls with the news that her teenager is in rehab, again.

Your phone beeps, and this text appears: "The doctor called. The cancer is back. Can we meet?"

From one moment to the next, you are invited into someone's hurt. You didn't volunteer; you were drafted. You didn't plan to discuss the death, divorce, or disease. But sometimes you have no choice.

I didn't. The woman just looked at me and said, "I'm getting older and sicker by the moment. I think God is done with me."

She and I shared a ride in a funeral limousine of all things. She was related to the deceased. I was a friend of the deceased. We'd both attended the memorial and were heading to the cemetery.

Trips to the cemetery have a way of reminding us of our own mortality. Maybe that's why she went unexpectedly verbal with her woes.

"Ever since I turned eighty, I've been so sick. I've prayed so much. I don't think I'm going to get better."

And then staring out the window at the winter sky, she repeated her conclusion. "I think God is done with me."

It wasn't a happy conversation. She wasn't a happy person. What do you say to someone who thinks God is MIA? Agree? Disagree? Say little? Say a lot?

The New Testament story of Lazarus reveals what Jesus would say. The story begins simply: "Now a certain man was sick, Lazarus of Bethany" (John 11:1).

I guess we all have to be known for something. Martha was bossy. Judas was greedy. Matthew had rowdy friends. And Lazarus? Well, Lazarus was sick.

Unfortunate but not unusual. Everyone gets sick. Lazarus's situation wasn't uncommon except for one detail. He had a pal named Jesus. He is described as Jesus' "dear friend" (v. 3 NLT).

This is a rare descriptor. Scripture describes people as Jesus' student, follower, family, antagonist, critic, but friend? A *dear* friend"?

Lazarus, apparently, genuinely liked Jesus. He liked his stories, his jokes. Others liked to be seen with Jesus or to be taught by Jesus. Not Lazarus. He just liked Jesus.

And Jesus liked Lazarus. It's wonderful to imagine Jesus spotting Lazarus at a busy luncheon, motioning for him to come over, and asking, "Want to hang out this week?" Friends spend time together. They share life. Jesus and Lazarus did this.

And now the friend of Jesus was sick. Very sick. So sick that his sisters, Mary and Martha, "sent a message to Jesus telling him, 'Lord, your dear friend is very sick'" (v. 3 NLT).

They surely assumed Jesus would come quickly. After all, they weren't unknown faces in the crowd. Their Bethany house was for all practical purposes his house. They kept his favorite tea in the cupboard. They knew the kind of cake he liked to eat on his birthday. They had every reason to think, *Jesus will drop whatever he is doing and hurry to help.*

Lazarus made the same assumption. He was desperate. He couldn't keep his food down. He couldn't stand up. Every joint ached. His head pounded like a bass drum. But he had this one assurance: "Jesus is on his way." He expected to hear Jesus' arrival at any moment. The scurry of feet. The welcome announcement from Mary: "You are here!" The concerned voice of Christ: "Where is Lazarus? Where's my friend?"

So in and out of feverish moments, as day became night and night became day, he asked Mary and Martha, "Any sign of Jesus? Is he here? Any word?"

Always the answer "No." No word. No sign. No message.

Lazarus, the dear, sick friend of Jesus, never heard back from him. He spent his final hours asking where Jesus was.

Does he care about me? Lazarus wondered.

Does he care about us? his sisters pondered.

"When Jesus arrived, he learned that Lazarus had already been dead and in the tomb for four days" (v. 17 EXB).

Not only did Jesus not make it to the deathbed of Lazarus, but he also didn't make it to the burial. Not only did he miss the burial, but he was also four days late.

Martha was forthright. "Lord, if only you had been here, my brother would not have died" (v. 21 NLT). Then she gathered herself. "But even now I know that God will give you whatever you ask" (v. 22 NLT).

Martha was distraught, brokenhearted. Martha was to Jesus what your hurting friend is to you. How can we respond when our friend is undone? When our neighbor despairs? When the woman in the funeral limousine thinks God has forgotten her? What do we do?

Here is what Jesus did. He looked Martha in the face and said these starchy words: "I am the resurrection and the life. . . . Do you believe this?" (vv. 25–26 NLT).

The Bible's word for such a response is *admonishment*. "Admonish one another," Paul told us (Rom. 15:14).

Admonishment is high-octane encouragement. The word literally means "putting in mind."[1] To admonish is to deposit truth into a person's thoughts. It might take the form of discipline, encouragement, or affirmation. It may be commendation or correction. Above all, admonishment is truth spoken into a difficult circumstance. It inserts the chlorine tablet of veracity into the algae of difficulty.

Admonishment speaks up.

Yes, we hold the hand of the struggler. Yes, we bring water to the thirsty. Yes, we prepare a meal for the hungry. And yes, yes, yes, we speak words of truth into moments of despair.

Dare we sit idly by while Satan spreads his lies? By no means! Unsheathe God's sword, the Word of God, and brandish its glimmering blade in the face of evil. "Finally, be strong in the Lord, and in the strength of his might. Put on the whole armor of God. . . . And take the helmet of salvation, and the sword of the Spirit, which is the word of God" (Eph. 6:10–11, 17 ASV).

When you read or quote a scripture in the face of pain or doubt or evil, you activate a weapon of the Spirit. It is as if a blade of God slashes against the rope of the Devil, and his prisoners are released. "His powerful Word is sharp as a surgeon's scalpel, cutting through everything, whether doubt or defense, laying us open to listen and obey. Nothing and no one is impervious to God's Word. We can't get away from it—no matter what" (Heb. 4:12–13 THE MESSAGE).

Scripture-based admonishment is like antibacterial cream. We may not know how it heals a wound; we just know it does.

Apply it and see what happens. Make it your practice to say, "I know a verse in the Bible that might help."

Or "A scripture that means much to me is . . ."

Or "May I read a Bible passage to you?"

My go-to list includes scriptures like these:

If God is for us, who can be against us? (Rom. 8:31 NIV)

He who has begun a good work in you will complete it. (Phil. 1:6)

I will never leave you nor forsake you. (Heb. 13:5)

After church last Sunday I met a ten-year-old boy by the name of Joshua. His mother, who was standing next to him, explained that Joshua's father was no longer a part of his son's life. The boy looked at me through sad, tear-moistened eyes. I squatted down eye level with Joshua and asked, "Do you know the story of your namesake?" He nodded. "You will do what he did," I admonished. "You will bring down Jericho's walls and pray prayers of great faith." He wasn't quite sure how to respond. But his mom? She was wiping her eyes.

Strugglers don't need our opinions. They don't need our philosophies on suffering. They don't need someone to distract them with idle conversation about weather or politics. They need someone to admonish them with truth.

My wife, Denalyn, excels at admonishment. Last evening I noticed she was texting back and forth with a friend who was spiraling downward because of some criticism at work. Denalyn encouraged her with this downpour of truth:

> Jesus can move mountains, so he can and will act on your behalf! He loves you, so receive his love and his power. Quit doubting the King of kings and Teacher of all teachers. Believe in him, and step in the resurrection power that is already yours in Christ Jesus. He is who he says. Believe him! The Lord exposes our weaknesses so we'll come to him and find our rest and hope in him. He wants you to come to him and stop imagining terrible scenarios. Has he not brought you this far? That's the Creator of the ends of the earth in your court, on your side. He is for you, not against you. Trust in him! Worship him! Take your position in praise and prayer, and he will set ambushes for the Enemy.

Goodness gracious, would that text not stir your spirit?

Spread words of hope, and pray prayers of faith. "Prayers offered in faith will restore them from sickness *and bring them to health*. The Lord will lift [the sick] up *from the floor of despair*" (James 5:15 THE VOICE).

The faith-filled prayer is a prayer of admonishment. The prayer of faith invites God to be God, to be sovereign over a tumultuous time.

Dennis McDonald models this type of admonishment. He was our church's hospital chaplain for many years. On occasions I accompanied him when he visited the sick. I was always struck by the transformation that came over him as he began to minister. We might be walking down a hospital hallway, chatting about the weather or a golf tournament, but when we entered the room, he went to work. He walked directly to the side of the hospital bed and leaned over until he was only inches from the face of the infirm. And he would say something like "I am Dennis, and I am here to pray for you and encourage you. God is greater than your sickness. God can heal your body. God will get you through this."

Dennis would then anoint the sick person with oil and pray, "Lord, this is your servant, whom you love and whom we love. Let your healing happen in this room. Satan, you must leave. You're a liar, and your words have no merit. This child is bought by God. We pray in Jesus' name, amen."

This is the job of the church: to take struggling followers and lead them back to the path of faith.

Some years ago I saw an example of this in a church service. We were studying the promise of Revelation 19:7.

> Let us be glad and rejoice,
> and let us give honor to him.
> For the time has come for the wedding feast of the Lamb,
> and his bride has prepared herself. (NLT)

As I was writing a sermon about the bride of Christ, I thought, *What better way to conclude the message than to invite a bride to enter?* Unbeknownst to the audience we recruited a volunteer and dressed her in a wedding gown and veil, a veil that covered her face. At the appropriate time I signaled for the music to start, the congregation to stand, the lights to dim, and the bride to begin her walk.

She did . . . straight into the back pew. I don't know how I expected her to do anything else; the veil blocked her vision. She gathered herself and set out again, only to walk into another pew. She could not stay on the path. She pinballed her way a few steps down the aisle before several people mercifully stepped out to guide her to the altar.

I intended to illustrate the beauty of the bride. In the end, however, we were given an illustration of our need for admonishment. We, too, sway from side to side. We, too, struggle to find our way. Each of us at one time or another needs someone to keep us on track.

We ended up with the bride standing at the altar and a half-dozen chuckling helpers at her side.

An image of what awaits us all, perhaps? When we stand at the altar of Christ on the final day, we will appreciate the influence of those who stepped out and spoke up to help us.

You can do this. Do not shrink back. After all, you are an ambassador for Christ. Can the ambassador stay silent? You are a child of God. Would a child not speak up for his father? You are a coheir with Christ. Can the heir remain silent while the blessings are available?

Of course not, so I didn't. Remember the woe-filled woman I told you about? She said, "I'm getting older and sicker by the moment. I think God is done with me." I was tempted to ignore the remark. I didn't know her. She scarcely knew me. Besides, there were other people in the funeral limousine. But something stirred me to speak. So I turned and looked at her. "Don't talk that way," I urged. "God isn't finished with you. He is your father. He loves you. He is your shepherd. He leads you. Your days were numbered before one of them came to be. You can't increase the quantity of your days, but you can affect their quality. You are in God's hands."

Her husband piped up. "That's what I've been telling her."

Tears filled her eyes. "Really?" she asked me.

"Really," I assured.

For a few moments no one spoke. The car entered the cemetery and came to a stop at the curb. As we stepped out, she resolved, "I'm going to trust God."

I pray that she did and that we will too.

After Jesus admonished Martha, he did the unthinkable. He went to the tomb, wept for his friend, and then shouted for the dead Lazarus to come out. And Lazarus did! He exited the tomb. But don't think for a second that Lazarus was the only miracle that day. Jesus resurrected the brother from the dead, but he also resurrected Martha's heart from despair. And he did both with words of power.

10

You've Been Bustered

Forgive one another as
quickly and thoroughly as
God in Christ forgave you.

—EPHESIANS 4:32 THE MESSAGE

This is the story of Buster. His name isn't Buster, but I need to keep his name private because my story isn't complimentary. Besides, the name fits him. He was a buster. In high school football he busted through offensive lines like a bulldozer. In baseball he busted baseball after baseball over the home-run fence.

Buster ruled our campus like a gang leader. He was raw and ripped; he had linebacker arms and a tiger snarl. Most of us avoided his orbit. But one Friday night I got caught up in it. Several of us were hanging out in a grocery store parking lot. Buster didn't like something I said or the way I said it. Emboldened by a belly of beer and a bunch of buddies, he came after me. He shoved me through the open door of a sedan and set out to reshape my jaw. Buster on Max was a grizzly on a squirrel. He pounded my face until some guys grabbed him by the ankles and pulled him off. I climbed out—eyes bruised, pride bruised even more—and walked away with my tail between my legs.

I spent the weekend trying to sort out his actions. What had I done wrong? Should I have fought back? Should I go find him? Was he looking for me? I plotted what I would say to him on Monday. It took some courage, but I mustered enough to catch him in the hallway between classes.

"Why did you jump me Friday night?"

He gave me a crooked, cocky grin. "Oh, I don't remember. I was drunk." And he walked off. The explanation hurt more than his fists had. I wasn't his enemy. I just happened to be the nearest punching bag.

I haven't seen Buster in decades. But I see his type almost weekly. When the young wife told me about her abusive husband, I thought of Buster. When I read about the kid who was bullied at high school, Buster came to mind. A corporation bought a small business, cleaned house, and fired everyone. Buster.

We all have a Buster. Or two or ten. Mine was a gadfly compared to yours. Your Buster was your dad; he came at you daily. Your Buster said, "I love you," when you were young and slender and "I don't want you" when you grew older and rounder. Your Buster flunked you out of spite. Your Buster cheated on you. Your Buster abandoned you.

You've been Bustered.

Maybe you've moved on. If not, a question needs to be raised regarding your happiness. Resentment sucks satisfaction from the soul. Bitterness consumes it. Revenge is a monster with a monstrous appetite. One act of retaliation is never enough. One pound of flesh is never enough. Left unchecked, grudges send us on a downward spiral.

Your Buster took much. Are you going to let him take even more? Brood at great risk. Is life sweeter when you are sour? Better when you are dour? Of course not.

"It is foolish to harbor a grudge" (Eccl. 7:9 GNT).

Some people abandon the path of forgiveness because they perceive it to be impossibly steep. So let's be realistic about the act. Forgiveness does not pardon the offense, excuse the misdeed, or ignore it. Forgiveness is not necessarily reconciliation. A reestablished relationship with the transgressor is not essential or always even possible. Even more, the phrase "forgive and forget" sets an unreachable standard. Painful memories are not like old clothing. They defy easy shedding.

Forgiveness is simply the act of changing your attitude toward the offender; it's moving from a desire to harm toward an openness to be at peace. A step in the direction of forgiveness is a decisive step toward happiness.

When researchers from Duke University listed eight factors that promote emotional stability, four of them related to forgiveness.

1. Avoiding suspicion and resentment.
2. Not living in the past.
3. Not wasting time and energy fighting conditions that can't be changed.
4. Refusing to indulge in self-pity when handed a raw deal.[1]

In a paper titled "Granting Forgiveness or Harboring Grudges," researchers relate how they invited people to reflect on a person who had caused them harm. Just the thought of the perpetrator led to sweaty palms, facial muscle tension, a higher heart rate, and increased blood pressure. When subjects were instructed to imagine the possibility of forgiveness, all the above physiological issues were reversed.[2] Health and happiness happen when forgiveness begins to flow.

It's no wonder then that the flotilla of "one another" scriptures includes one named the *USS Forgiveness*. "Be kind to one another, tenderhearted, forgiving one another, even as God in Christ forgave you" (Eph. 4:32).

There goes the apostle Paul doing it again. It was not enough for him to say, "Forgive one another as your conscience dictates." Or "to the degree that you feel comfortable." Or "as much as makes common sense." No, Paul did what he loved to do: he used Jesus as our standard. Forgive others as Christ forgave you.

So we leave the Epistles and thumb our way leftward into the Gospels, looking for a time in which Jesus forgave others. We are barely through the back entrance to John's gospel before we find an example. The story includes a basin of water, a towel, two dozen sweaty feet, and one dozen disciples.

> Jesus, knowing that the Father had given all things into His hands, and that He had come from God and was going to God, rose from supper and laid aside His garments, took a towel and girded Himself. After that, He poured water into a basin and began to wash the disciples' feet, and to wipe them with the towel with which He was girded. (John 13:3–5)

This was the eve of the crucifixion and Jesus' final meal with his followers. John wanted us to know what Jesus knew. Jesus knew he had all authority. He knew he was sent from heaven. He knew he was destined for heaven. Jesus was certain about his identity and destiny. Because he knew who he was, he could do what he did.

He "rose from supper" (v. 4). When Jesus stood up, the disciples surely perked up. They may have thought Jesus was about to teach them something. He was, but not with words.

He then "laid aside His garments" (v. 4). Even the simple, seamless garment of a rabbi was too ostentatious for the task at hand.

Jesus hung his cloak on a hook and girded the towel around his waist. He then took a pitcher of water and emptied it into a bowl. The only sound was the splash as Jesus filled the basin.

The next sound was the tap of the bowl as Jesus placed it on the floor. Then the shuffle of leather as he untied and removed the first of the two dozen sandals. There was more splashing as Jesus placed two feet, dirty as they were, into the water. He massaged the toes. He cupped crusty heels in his hands. He dried the feet with his towel. He then stood, emptied the basin of dirty water, filled it with fresh, and repeated the process on the next set of feet.

Splash. Wash. Massage. Dry.

How much time do you think this cleansing required? Supposing Jesus took two or three minutes per foot, this act would have taken the better part of an hour. Keep in mind, Jesus was down to his final minutes with his followers. If his three years with them were measured by sand in an hourglass, only a few grains had yet to fall. Jesus chose to use them in this silent sacrament of humility.

No one spoke. No one, that is, except Peter, who always had something to say. When he objected, Jesus insisted, going so far as to tell Peter, "If I do not wash you, you have no part with Me" (v. 8).

Peter requested a bath.

Later that night the disciples realized the enormity of this gesture. They had pledged to stay with their Master, but those pledges melted like wax in the heat of the Roman torches. When the soldiers marched in, the disciples ran out.

I envision them sprinting until, depleted of strength, they plopped to the ground and let their heads fall forward as they looked wearily at the dirt. That's when they saw the feet Jesus had just washed. That's when they realized he had given them grace before they even knew they needed it.

Jesus forgave his betrayers before they betrayed him.

Hasn't he done the same for us? Yes, we each have a Buster, but we also have a basin. We've been wounded, perhaps deeply. But haven't we been forgiven preemptively? Before we knew we needed grace, we were offered it.

Heaven must have a basin warehouse that contains row after row of ceramic bowls. Each bowl has a name affixed to it. One particularly well-worn basin bears the name Max. Every day, multiple times a day, Jesus sends an angel to fetch it. "Lucado needs another cleansing." The angel wings his way over to the warehouse and informs the manager. "Again?" asks the supervisor. "Again," affirms the angel. The angel retrieves it and carries it to Christ. The Master takes my container, fills it with cleansing grace, and washes away my sins. All my betrayals sink like silt to the bottom of the bowl. Jesus throws them out.

Have you considered how often he washes you?

Suppose I were somehow to come into possession of your sin-history video. Every contrary act. Every wayward thought. Every reckless word. Would you want me to play it on a screen? By no means. You'd beg me not to. And I would beg you not to show mine.

Don't worry. I don't have it. But Jesus does. He's seen it. He's seen every backstreet, back-seat, backhanded moment of our lives. And he has resolved, "My grace is enough. I can cleanse these people. I will wash away their betrayals." For that reason we must make the Upper Room of Mercy our home address.

The apostle John championed this thought of Christ's perpetual cleansing:

"But if we live in the light, as God is in the light, we can share fellowship with each other. Then the blood of Jesus, God's Son, cleanses us from every sin" (1 John 1:7 NCV).

"He can be depended on to forgive us and to cleanse us from every wrong" (1 John 1:9 TLB).

Christ, our cleanser. He knew our promises would fall like broken glass. He knew we would dart into a dark alley of shame. He knew we would bury our faces between our knees.

It is in this context that Paul urged us to follow Jesus' lead. To give grace rather than get retribution. To give grace, not because our Busters deserve it but because we've been doused with it. "Forgiving one another, even as God in Christ forgave you" (Eph. 4:32).

Wearing the towel and holding the basin, he said to his church, "This is how we do it."

"If I then, your Lord and Teacher, have washed your feet, you also ought to wash one another's feet. For I have given you an example, that you should do as I have done to you" (John 13:14–15).

Let others bicker and fight; we don't.

Let others seek revenge; we don't.

Let others keep a list of offenders; we don't.

We take the towel. We fill the basin. We wash one another's feet.

Jesus could do this because he knew who he was—sent from and destined for heaven. And you? Do you know who you are? You are the creation of a good God, made in his image. You are destined to reign in an eternal kingdom. You are only heartbeats away from heaven.

Secure in who you are, you can do what Jesus did. Throw aside the robe of rights and expectation and make the most courageous of moves. Wash feet.

Let's be "tenderhearted, forgiving one another" (Eph. 4:32).

Tenderhearted: malleable, soft, kind, responsive.

Hard-hearted: cold, stony, unbending.

Which words describe your heart?

A friend's nephew recently purchased a brand-new home. He was thrilled. New marriage, new job, new life. Things were looking up until foundation issues were discovered. The builder found a leak in the slab. A plumber jackhammered a large hole in one of their bathrooms to reach and repair the leaking pipe. The foundation repair company proceeded to tunnel under the house and backfill the hole with a concrete substance. They filled and filled. One truckload was not enough, so they emptied a second into the hole.

When the homeowner returned from work, he couldn't get the door open. It was soon discovered that the jackhammered area of the bathroom had never been closed. The truckloads of concrete had been emptied, not just into the foundation but also into the residence. When my friend's nephew was finally able to enter the house, he found the furniture cemented to the floor, and the toilet looked as if it were made for someone with no legs. He could rest his arm on the molding of a nine-foot-tall doorway.

Their house hardened while they weren't watching.

The same can happen to hearts. To be clear, my aim is not to dismiss a perpetrator or downplay your pain. The question is not, Did you get hurt? The question is, Are you going to let the hurt harden you? Numb you? Suck up all your joy?

Wouldn't you prefer to be "tenderhearted, forgiving one another"?

Try these steps.

Decide what you need to forgive. Get specific. Narrow it down to the identifiable offense. "He was a jerk" does not work. "He promised to leave his work at work and be attentive at home." There, that's better.

Ask yourself why it hurts. Why does this offense sting? What about it leaves you wounded? Do you feel betrayed? Ignored? Isolated? Do your best to find the answer, and before you take it out on the offender . . .

Take it to Jesus. No one will ever love you more than he does. Let this wound be an opportunity to draw near to your Savior. Does this experience and lack of forgiveness hamper your well-being? Does it diminish your peace? If the answer is yes, take steps in the direction of forgiveness. Talk to Jesus about the offense until the anger subsides. And when it returns, talk to Jesus again.

And *if it feels safe,* at some point . . .

Tell your offender. With a clear head and pure motives, file a complaint. Be specific. Not overly dramatic. Simply explain the offense and the way it makes you feel. It might sound something like this: "We agreed to make our home a haven. Yet after dinner you seem to get lost in emails and projects. Consequently, I feel lonely under my own roof."

If done respectfully and honestly, this is a step toward forgiveness. There is nothing easy about broaching a sensitive topic. You are putting on a servant's garb. By bringing it up you are giving forgiveness a chance to have its way and win the day.

Will it? Will grace triumph? There is no guarantee. Whether it does or not, your next step is to . . .

Pray for your offender. You cannot force reconciliation, but you can offer intercession. "Pray for those who persecute you" (Matt. 5:44 NIV). Prayer reveals any lingering grudge, and what better place to see it! You are standing before the throne of grace yet finding it difficult to give grace? Ask Jesus to help you.

Here is one final idea:

Conduct a funeral. Bury the offense. I don't mean to bury it in the sense of suppressing it. Nothing is gained by shoving negative emotions into your spirit. But something wonderful is gained by taking the memory, placing it in a casket (a shoebox will suffice), and burying it in the cemetery known as "Moving On with Life." Take off your hat, cover your heart, and shed one final tear. When the anger surfaces again, just tell yourself, "It's time to walk boldly into a bright future."

Many years ago a man came to see me regarding his wife's boss. As her supervisor, he overreached his bounds, demanding extra work and offering poor compensation. The husband confronted the man. To the credit of the supervisor, he owned up to his mismanagement and made amends.

The wife was grateful. But the husband was still angry. Chalk it up to a husband's intense desire to protect, but he could not forgive the man. So he came up with an idea that included a letter. He brought it to my office along with a box of matches. (I was a bit concerned when I saw the matches.) He read the letter to me. It was addressed to his offender and contained an account of the actions.

The husband then asked me to pray and watch as he burned the letter "before my anger burns me up." We did.

You might try the same.

Forgiveness is the act of applying your undeserved mercy to your undeserved hurts. You didn't deserve to be hurt, but neither did you deserve to be forgiven. Being the recipient that you are of God's great grace, does it not make sense to give grace to others?

General Oglethorpe once said to John Wesley, "I never forgive and I never forget." To which Wesley replied, "Then, Sir, I hope you never sin."[3]

You've not been sprinkled with forgiveness. You've not been spattered with grace. You've not been dusted with kindness. You've been immersed in forgiveness, submerged in grace. Can you, standing as you are, shoulder-high in God's ocean of grace, not fill a cup and offer the happiness of forgiveness to others?

During the season I wrote this book, the world watched in horror as twenty-one Christians were martyred for their faith by ISIS terrorists. Two of the slain men were brothers, ages twenty-three and twenty-five.

In an interview, a third brother was asked about his feelings regarding the loss of his siblings. He said:

> "ISIS helped us strengthen our faith. I thank ISIS because they didn't cut the audio when [my brothers] screamed declaring their faith."
>
> He was asked what his mother would do if she saw the ISIS member who killed her sons.
>
> "She said she would invite him home because he helped us enter the kingdom of heaven. These were my mother's words."[4]

Let's do likewise.

Happiness happens when you offer to others the grace you've been given. It's time to follow the example of Jesus in the Upper Room. It's time to forgive, just as God, in Christ, forgave you.

11

Be Loved,
Then Love

Love one another.

—1 JOHN 4:11

For decades Andrea Mosconi followed the same routine six mornings a week. The Italian maestro donned a coat and tie, went to the city hall in Cremona, Italy, and entered the violin museum. There he stood before the elaborate, multilocked cases and admired some of the most valuable musical instruments on the planet. They are to music what the Declaration of Independence is to American history: relics of inestimable value.

The museum contained two violins and a viola built by the Amati family, two violins by the Guarneris, and most precious of all a violin crafted by the hands of the master himself, Antonio Stradivari.

With most of them being more than three hundred years old, they deserve attention. Left untouched, untuned, and unstroked, the instruments begin to lose their vibrancy. Hence, Mr. Mosconi. His job description consisted of one sentence: play music. Every morning but Sunday and every month but August, he brought the best out of the best.

He gingerly and reverently removed each instrument from its glass case, played it for six or seven minutes, and then returned it before moving on to the next one. By the time he finished a day's work, the museum had heard the sweetest music, and the most valuable instruments had felt the tenderest care.[1]

You, me, and Mr. Mosconi have something in common. You don't step into a museum in Italy every day. I don't cradle a Stradivarius. We aren't conservators for musical instruments. No, our assignments are far more important. We have a chance to bring the best out of people. What could produce more joy than that?

Some of the treasures live in your house; they share your name. You tend to think of them as the ones who forget to clean the dishes or pick up their laundry. But the truth? They are finely tuned instruments crafted by the hand of God. You seldom regard them as such. After all, they have bad breath and bad attitudes and are prone to practice bad habits. But handled with care, they can make some music.

Your museum includes a host of functional folk as well. They check out your groceries, grade your quizzes, or take your blood pressure. They wear police uniforms and drive carpools and check your computer when the office internet goes down. They compose a collage of humanity, blending in more than standing out. They'd blush at the thought of being called a Stradivarius, yet that is what they are. Uniquely shaped and destined to bring one-of-a-kind music into the world.

All they need is a Mosconi, a skilled curator committed to bringing the best out of them. All they need is someone who is willing to take on the greatest of the "one another" commands: "Love one another" (1 John 4:11).

Remember, God invites us to find happiness through the back door. Most people seek joy through the front door. Buy it, wear it, marry it, or win it. The lesser-used back door embraces God's wisdom: happiness happens as we give it away. It's less about getting, more about giving, less about being loved, and more about loving others.

I find at least eleven appearances of the "love one another" admonition. Three by Christ (John 13:34; 15:12, 17). Three by Paul (Rom. 13:8;

1 Thess. 3:12; 4:9). One by Peter (1 Peter 1:22) and four by the apostle John (1 John 3:11; 4:7, 11; 2 John v. 5).

The Greek word used for *love* (*agape*) in these passages denotes an unselfish affection.[2] *Agape* love writes the check when the balance is low, forgives the mistake when the offense is high, offers patience when stress is abundant, and extends kindness when kindness is rare. "For God so loved [*agapaó*] the world that he gave his one and only Son" (John 3:16 NIV). *Agape* love gives. The *agape* tree is rooted in the soil of devotion. But don't think for a moment that its fruit is sour. A sweet happiness awaits those who are willing to care for the orchard.

Do you find such love difficult to muster? Scarce? If so, you may be missing a step. Love for others begins, not by giving love but by receiving the love of Christ. "A new commandment I give to you, that you love one another; as I have loved you" (John 13:34).

The final phrase is the essential one: "as I have loved you." Have you let God love you? Please don't hurry past the question. Have you let God's love seep into the innermost recesses of your life? Have you, as John wrote, "come to know [by . . . experience], and have believed . . . the love which God has for us" (1 John 4:16 AMP)?

If your answer is "Uh, I don't know" or "Well, it's been a while" or "I don't think God loves a person like me," then we just stumbled upon something.

We don't love people because people are lovable. (Only the husband of my wife is always lovable.) People can be cranky, stubborn, selfish, and cruel. We love people for this reason: *we have come to experience and believe the love that God has for us*. We are beneficiaries of an unexpected, undeserved, yet undeniable gift—the love of God.

We tend to skip this step. "I'm supposed to love my neighbor? All right, by golly, I will." We clinch our teeth and redouble our efforts as if there were within us a distillery of affection. If we poke it and prod it and turn up the heat, another bottle of love will pour forth.

It won't! The source is not within us. It is only by receiving our Father's *agape* love that we can discover an *agape* love for others.

Be loved. Then love. We cannot love if we aren't first loved. Just as hurt people hurt people, loved people love people.

So let God love you!

Discover the purest source of happiness, the love of God. A love that is "too wonderful to be measured" (Eph. 3:19 CEV). A love that is not regulated by the receiver. What Moses said to Israel is what God says to us: "The LORD did not set his heart on you and choose you because you were more numerous than other nations, for you were the smallest of all nations! Rather, it was simply that the LORD loves you" (Deut. 7:7–8 NLT).

Does he love us because of our goodness? Because of our kindness? Because of our great devotion? No, he loves us because of his goodness, kindness, and great devotion.

The reason God loves you is that he has chosen to love you.

You are loved when you don't feel lovely. You are loved by God even when you are loved by no one else. Others may abandon you, divorce you, and ignore you. God will love you. These are his words: "I'll call nobodies and make them somebodies; I'll call the unloved and make them beloved" (Rom. 9:25 THE MESSAGE).

Let this love happen in your life. Let this love give birth to the greatest joy: "I am beloved by heaven."

We must start here. Settle yourself into the hammock of God's affection. And as you do, to the degree you do, you will give that love to others.

Perhaps names of people who are anything but lovable are surfacing in your mind. Maybe you've spent a decade cultivating a stubborn bias against him or nursing a grudge against her or indulging a pet prejudice against them.

Prepare yourself for a new day. As God has his way with you, as he loves through you, those old animosities and barbed-wire fences are going to come down. That's how happiness happens. God will not let you live with your old hatred and prejudices. Remember, "If anyone is in Christ, he is a new creation; old things have passed away; behold, all things have become new" (2 Cor. 5:17).

As God's love flows through you, you will see people in a different way. "From this time on we do not think of anyone as the world does" (2 Cor. 5:16 NCV).

You have God living inside you. Maybe you have had trouble loving the homeless. God can love them through you. Perhaps your friends taught you to bully the weak or slander the rich. God will create a new attitude. He indwells you.

The woman at the grocery counter? She is not just an employee; she is fearfully and wonderfully made.

The husband at the breakfast table? He is not just a fellow who needs a shave; he is God's creation, destined for a heavenly assignment.

The neighbor down the street? He's not a person who forgets to mow his lawn. He is made in the image of God.

God will plant in your heart an appreciation for his multifaceted family. Self-centeredness wants a uniform world: everyone looking alike, acting alike. God loves a diverse creation. "We are His workmanship" (Eph. 2:10). The word *workmanship* comes from the Greek word *poiéma*, which could be translated "poetry."[3] We are the poetry of God! What Longfellow did with pen and paper, our Maker has done with us. We are an expression of his creative best.

We are his poetry. You aren't God's poetry. I'm not God's poetry.

Together we are God's poetry. Independently we are nothing but small pieces on God's page. You may be a verb, she may be a noun, and I'm probably a question mark. We're just letters, marks from God's hand.

What letter, then, has a right to criticize another? Dare the *p* accuse the *q* of being backward? Dare the *m* mock the *w* for being too open minded? Who are we to tell the writer how to form us or when to use us? We need each other. By ourselves we are just letters on a page, but collectively we are poetry.

Agape love finds beauty in the collage of humanity. Logical thinkers. Emotional worshipers. Dynamic leaders. Docile followers. The gregarious who greet, the studious who ponder, the generous who pay the bills. Apart from each other we have an incomplete message, but together "we are His workmanship" (Eph. 2:10).

Imagine the joy you will find as you learn to find joy in people. (Might as well. They are everywhere!) Life will become less a chore and more a stroll through God's art gallery.

Just yesterday I found myself sharing a golf cart with a sixty-plus-year-old fellow I'd never met. We ended up on the same California course hoping to cash in on a blue sky and make a par or two. As he shared his story, I realized he has every reason to be miserable. He has battled migraines for twenty years, lost a wife through divorce, is currently between jobs, and has had to move at least once a year for the last decade.

Yet to hear him talk, you'd think he just danced Dorothy down the yellow brick road. Can't credit his golf game. His swing was a bit wayward. But his happiness was contagious. He had me smiling from tee box to sand trap. I had to ask him, "For a fellow with so many bad breaks in life, how is it that you smile all the time?"

He looked at me with sparkling eyes. "I get to meet people! Each human is a story. How can you not love a world when it is so full of stories!"

My friend understands how happiness happens.

Let's invite the Father to kindle an equal fascination in our hearts. Think about it. If every person is a reason for joy, we have seven billion reasons to smile.

Keep in mind, we are all works in progress. You wouldn't pass judgment on the wine of a vineyard after eating only one grape or pass an opinion on the work of an artist after one brushstroke. You give the vineyard time to mature and the artist an opportunity to complete the painting.

Give God the same. He isn't finished, and some of his works—well, some of us—need extra attention. Take a cue from the apostle Paul, who told some friends:

> There has never been the slightest doubt in my mind that the God who started this great work in you would keep at it and bring it to a flourishing finish on the very day Christ Jesus appears. (Phil. 1:6 THE MESSAGE)

God isn't finished yet. Let the grapes mature. Give the artist some time. Applaud the progress you see. Be the cheerleader who brings out the best, not the critic who points out the rest. You'll enjoy the relationship, and so will they.

Embrace your role as a Mr. Mosconi. See your world as a museum of divine treasures. See yourself as their caretaker. You exist to draw the music out of them. Mosconi had a closet of tools: rosin, oils, and violin bows. You have a tool chest as well: encouraging words, a phrase of admonition, a warm greeting, genuine forgiveness. You rosin your relationships with patience and kindness and unselfishness. You do whatever it takes to bring out the best in others.

Why? Because God is bringing out the best in you. Little by little, day after day, from one degree of glory to the next, God is making a new you out of you. Don't give in to this itty-bitty, negative-thought committee that relegates you to the side of the road. Maybe you've failed at love. No matter. God gives second chances. Perhaps you've earned a reputation as a snark. No problem. God can change that. He can change you. He hasn't given up on you. Don't give up on yourself.

I had granddaddy duty the other night. Rosie's parents had an obligation, and my wife was out of town, so guess who had a date with his two-and-a-half-year-old sweetheart? Oh, the time we had. She dressed up in a wedding gown. We ate Cheerios with no milk. We danced to Disney music. And to top it off we walked to the gate in the dark.

Our house is a ten-minute walk from our front gate. For Rosie the journey is a Lewis and Clark–level adventure. As we began the trek, she held up her hand like a crosswalk guard halting a jaywalker. "Stay there, Papa Max. I go by myself."

I paused. I lingered back just far enough to let her think she was on her own. You and I know I would never let her walk to the gate by herself. Especially at 9:00 p.m.

After a few steps she stopped and looked around. Maybe it was the sound of rustling leaves. Or the shadows falling across the path. I do not know why she stopped. But I was close enough to see her do so. And close enough to hear her say, "Papa Max!"

I was at her side in two seconds. She looked up at me and smiled. "Come with me?" We walked the rest of the way hand in hand.

We preachers tend to overcomplicate this thing of God's love. We fixate on long words and theological thoughts when perhaps the best illustration is something like Rosie walking in the dark, crying out for help, and her Papa hurrying to oblige.

Your Father is following you, my friend. And on this journey of life and love, when the night strikes more fear than faith, when you find it impossible to love the people who are hard to love, just pause and call his name. He's nearer than you might think. And he's not about to let you walk this path without his help.

The Next Step

The Happiness Challenge

The biggest moment in the history of the University of Southern California football does not include a trophy hoist or a touchdown dash. In my opinion the event that deserves a spot in the Hall of Fame includes no game-winning pass or Gatorade-drenched coach. If given the chance to stand on the sidelines and watch one moment of the storied program that began in 1880, I would select 2017, USC versus Western Michigan. With three minutes and thirteen seconds to go in the fourth quarter, USC intercepted a pass for a touchdown and took a solid 48–31 lead. A few of the 61,125 fans began walking toward the Los Angeles Memorial Coliseum exits. The rest of the game, it appeared, was a formality.

But then head coach Clay Helton shouted for Jake Olson, a redshirt sophomore, to take the field to deep-snap the football for the extra point.

What makes the moment historic and unforgettable is not that a player was called off the bench. The unique stand-up-and-watch-thisness of the play was that the player was blind. That's right. Jake Olson trotted onto a field that was, to him, cast in midnight black. He could not see the smiling faces of the other Trojans in the huddle. He was unable to see the row of teammates on the sideline, all standing, all watching. He had no vision of the coaches who, with blurry eyes and tight throats, knew they were watching a dream come true.

Jake Olson's journey toward this game began at the age of ten months, when he lost his left eye to retinal cancer. The cancer returned when he was twelve years old. Doctors determined that the only way to contain the cancer was to remove the right eye also.

Pete Carroll was the USC head coach at the time. A mutual friend of the Olson family told him about a boy who was a lifelong Trojan fan and about to lose his sight. Carroll set out to fill Jake's head with USC football memories: he arranged for Jake to meet players, participate in pre- and post-practice huddles, and hold the traditional band leader's sword and direct the band after a game. Jake even traveled to Notre Dame with the team.

Then came the darkness.

When he was healthy enough to attend a team practice after the surgery, he was welcomed as if he'd won the Heisman.

When Carroll took a job with the Seattle Seahawks, he invited Olson to join his team on the sidelines for a game. That's when the center for the team asked Olson if he'd ever deep-snapped a football. Blindness could keep Olson from throwing, tackling, blocking, and catching, but launching the ball between his legs to a holder eight yards away? Olson learned to do it. He made it his dream to play in at least one USC game.

To make it happen, the coaches of the two teams had to talk. The Western Michigan squad agreed not to crush Olson with a rushing linebacker. The USC coaching staff agreed to use Olson only after the game was out of reach for one of the two teams. The school cleared the decision with the Pac-12 conference. Jake suited up and awaited his opportunity.

For most of the game Olson's moment was in doubt. The score was 14–14 at half, 21–21 after three quarters. With six minutes to go in the game, the teams were knotted at 28–28. But then USC caught fire, scored three times, and put the game away.

Coach Helton called time-out. Olson took a couple of practice snaps. While he warmed up, Helton signaled to the Western Michigan coach, who signaled to his team. Every player on both sides of the field perked up. The official, also in on the drama, spotted the ball, placed a hand on Olson's back, stepped out of the way, and whistled for the play to begin.

At that moment there were no competitors, no opposing sides, no winners and losers. There was only one player overcoming a massive handicap, and everyone rooted for him.

In the history of college football, the game was but one of thousands. The moment, however, was one in a million. On cue Olson spiraled a perfect snap. The ball was placed, the kick was good, and Jake was mobbed by his teammates.

It was, perhaps, the greatest extra point in the history of the Trojans.[1]

Don't we love stories like that? What word captures the way such moments make us feel? How about this one: *happy.*

And we weren't even there! I wasn't in the stands. Odds are, you weren't on the field. We didn't see the snap or witness the kick, yet it makes us happy just to read about it.

Happiness has a way of cascading forth when humanity is unselfish enough to help others have their moment.

Gratefully, we can replicate such moments any time of the day and any place on earth. Desire a rain shower of joy? Weary of the drudgery of the day to day? Then do this: serve someone, greet someone, give up your seat, listen to someone's story, write a check, pen a letter, give your time, your counsel, and your heart.

Make someone happy.

"It is more blessed to give than to receive" (Acts 20:35).

It is better to forgive than to hold a grudge,

... better to build up than to tear down,
... better to include than to exclude,
... better to seek to understand than to disregard,
... better to love than to hate.

God's solution for the ills of society is a quorum of unselfish, life-giving, God-loving folks who flow through neighborhoods and businesses like cleansing agents, bringing in the good, flushing out the bad. They hail from all corners of the globe, reflect all hues of skin. Liberal, conservative, rural, metropolitan, young, old. Yet they are bound together by this amazing discovery: happiness is found by giving it away.

If anyone is happier than the gift receiver, it is the gift giver.

Albert can tell you. He is a mail carrier in Waco, Texas. He makes daily deliveries to the furniture store where my daughter Sara used to work. The store was wildly successful. Being a start-up, the business had a constant level of chaos. Everyone was learning the system at the same time. Employees were on their feet all day. It could be a stressful place.

That's why they all loved Albert. Sara described his arrival as the high point of the day. The high point! She remembers, "He'd ask how each of us was doing. He looked us in the eyes and said, 'God bless you.'"

Albert delivers more than mail. He delivers happiness.

I'd like to challenge you to do the same. Here is my idea. Set out to alter the joy level of a hundred people over the next forty days. Intentionally put into practice the "one another" passages. Pray for people, serve more, practice patience, and bring the best out in people. Keep a journal in which you describe the encounter and what you did. Make note of the moment. What was the setting? What did you learn?

THE NEXT STEP: THE HAPPINESS CHALLENGE

At the end of forty days, would your world be different?

Would you be different?

I certainly am. I took the challenge as I wrote this book. The experience was twice as difficult as I imagined but a hundred times more fulfilling than I ever thought it would be.

Here is a typical entry from my journal:

The plane departing Minneapolis was two hours late due to—as the gate attendant announced to the passengers in the waiting area—"Flight crew delay." By the time the three flight attendants appeared, the hour was nearing bedtime. They were tired from a previous flight and were sheepish as they passed through a crowd of grim-faced passengers. Someone actually booed them.

When we finally boarded, it was still chaotic. There was not enough overhead space. Too many winter coats. I ended up placing my bag a football field away from my seat. I sat down with a sigh. Then I remembered the "Hundred Happy People Challenge." About half an hour into the flight I had an opportunity to thank the flight attendant for the professional way in which she handled the delay. She appreciated my thanks. Yet I felt I could do more. Midway through the flight I got up from my seat and walked to her workstation.

"I want to say again I really appreciate your work."

This time she stopped. Tears filled her eyes. "That means a lot. It has been a long day."

Want to give the happiness challenge a try?

Everyone else shows up at work with a scowl and a list of things to get done. But you? You still have your work to accomplish, but you also have this pursuit. Whom can I help today? Which person can I encourage? Who needs a little sunshine?

Maybe the new employee who occupies the cubicle down the hall. Or the neighbor whose Chihuahua wanders into your yard. Or your teacher. Yes, your teacher. The one who sucks lemons for breakfast and devours students for lunch. Others avoid her. Not you. You look for ways to lift her spirits, brighten her day, compliment her, understand her, thank her. Will the world be different because you tried?

You bet your sweet September it will.

You will become the equivalent of an ice cream truck in your world. An ice cream truck used to visit my childhood neighborhood. To this day, a half century later, if a band plays "When the Saints Go Marching In," my mouth begins to water, and I search my pockets for a nickel. When I heard the clanking music of the truck, I knew what to do.

I wasn't alone. Kids came from everywhere. Little League parks. Backyards. Schoolyards. Houses disgorged youngsters the way subways unload passengers. They pedaled their bikes, shoved their scooters, or just ran like crazy. The ice cream truck was in the neighborhood.

Be that ice cream truck. Be the person that people are glad to see. Be the voice people want to hear. Drive the happiness truck.

And see if you aren't the one smiling the most.

Questions for Reflection

Prepared by Andrea Lucado

1

The Unexpected Door to Joy

1. How would you define happiness? What words, feelings, or images come to mind when you think about being happy?

2. Describe a time in your life when you were happy. What made this a happy time?

3. Identify a time in your life when you were unhappy. What made this an unhappy time?

4. Assess your current happiness level. Do you feel happy most days, some days, or hardly ever? Why? What is the primary source of your happiness or unhappiness?

5. Max writes, "Worldwide, people profess that happiness is their most cherished goal" (p. 4). Is this true for you? Why or why not?

6. This chapter includes several startling statistics regarding the current state of happiness in our world:
   Only one-third of Americans surveyed claimed to be happy.
   Clinical depression is ten times more common now than it was a century ago.

___

The World Health Organization predicts that by 2020 "depression will become the second leading cause of disease worldwide" (p. 5).

- Do these statistics surprise you? Why or why not?
- Are you currently dealing with depression, or have you ever struggled with depression? If so, how would you describe that journey?
- Has a close friend or family member ever been challenged by depression? What did you observe as you walked with this person on his or her journey?
- Why do you think depression is so common today?

7. Max describes the "front door to happiness" as something that advertisers sell: wealth, appearance, sex, and possessions (p. 6).
   - What front-door promises of happiness have you bought into in the past?
   - Did those promises deliver what you wanted? Why or why not?
   - Which front-door promises are you pursuing today?
   - Are they delivering what you hoped for? Why or why not?
   - Over your life—childhood, adolescence, adulthood—how has your quest for front-door happiness changed?

8. Fill in the blanks. The motto on the front door to happiness is "Happiness happens when you _____." The motto on the lesser-used door to happiness is "Happiness happens when you _____."
   - What was your reaction when you first read the motto for the lesser-used door?
   - Do you agree with it? Why or why not?

---

9. Toward the end of the book of Acts, when Paul said farewell to the church in Ephesus, he told them, "Remember the words of the Lord Jesus, that He said, 'It is more blessed to give than to receive'" (Acts 20:35). The Christian life is full of paradoxes like this. Read Matthew 5:1–12. The Greek word translated as *blessed* can also be translated as *happy*. With this in mind answer the following questions.

   - According to Jesus, who are the happy people?
   - What does this passage tell us about God's idea of happiness versus the world's idea?
   - Have you ever encountered someone who by worldly standards did not have what a person needs to be happy—wealth, prestige, or beauty—and was happy nonetheless?
   - Why do you think he or she was so happy?
   - How did interacting with that person affect you?

10. Max points out that Scripture describes Jesus as joyful, the type of person people liked to be around and the type of person who was always up for a party.

   - We often describe Jesus as wise, truthful, sacrificial, and loving, but have you ever described Jesus as happy, as a person who smiled, laughed, and enjoyed parties?
   - How do you react to the idea of Jesus being happy, attending parties, smiling, and laughing? Does it make you uncomfortable? Why or why not?
   - What made Jesus happy?

11. Fill in the blank: If we are going to find true happiness, we must ____ it away.

---

12. Max lists ten "one another" verses that can teach us how to give happiness away and experience it for ourselves as a result.

    Encourage one another (1 Thess. 5:11).

    Bear with one another (Eph. 4:2).

    Regard one another as more important (Phil. 2:4).

    Greet one another (Rom. 16:16).

    Pray for one another (James 5:16).

    Serve one another (Gal. 5:13).

    Accept one another (Rom. 15:7).

    Admonish one another (Col. 3:16).

    Forgive one another (Eph. 4:32).

    Love one another (1 John 3:11).

    - Of these ten "one another" verses, which one do you believe you do best?
    - Which one do you most need to work on?

13. Where would you most like to see a "quiet revolution of joy" break out—in your home, community, workplace, or the nation? Identify which "one another" verse you could use to help start that quiet revolution.

2

Gimme Five, Rocky

1. In 1 Thessalonians 5:9–11 while addressing the church at Thessalonica, Paul wrote, "For God did not appoint us to suffer wrath but to receive salvation through our Lord Jesus Christ. He died for us so that, whether we are awake or asleep, we may live together with him. Therefore encourage one another and build each other up, just as in fact you are doing" (NIV).
   - According to this passage, why do we encourage one another and build up each other?
   - What is the difference, if any, between encouraging each other and encouraging each other in Christ?

2. The Greek word for *encouragement* is *parakaleo*.[1]
   - What does *para* mean in the Greek, and what does *kaleo* mean?
   - Based on these meanings, how did Jesus intend for us to encourage other people?

3. Jesus exemplified this type of encouragement when Peter said that he believed Jesus was the Son of the living God.
   - How did Jesus respond to Peter in Matthew 16:17?
   - How would you feel if Jesus encouraged you in this way?

---

4. Max cites a study that found "healthy homes enjoy a positive-to-negative ratio of five to one" (p. 19).
   - What would you estimate is the ratio of positive to negative comments in your home, workplace, or circle of friends?
   - If you tend to hear or say more negative comments, why do you think that is the case?
   - If you tend to hear or say more positive comments, why do you think that is the case?

5. In what area of your life have you experienced a "discouragement conspiracy"? On social media? In the news? With your family, friends, or church?
   - How has this discouragement affected you personally?
   - How has it affected the way you view the world and others?

6. Look up the following verses: 2 Corinthians 12:9; Galatians 4:7; Ephesians 1:7; 1 Peter 2:9.
   - What do these verses say about who we are in Christ?
   - How could these truths help you fight the discouragement conspiracy?
   - Which one of these do you need to focus on to encourage yourself today?
   - Which one of these could you use to encourage someone else?

7. Max lists two ways we can encourage others in order to "call forth the Rocky within them" (p. 22–24). First, we listen intently.
   - How can listening encourage someone?
   - How do you think the bleeding woman in Mark 5:33 felt as she told Jesus her story and he listened?

- When a friend confides in you, what is your reaction? Are you quick to speak, or do you primarily listen? Why is this your reaction?
- When was the last time someone listened intently to you? How did that make you feel?
- Identify a person you could encourage by listening intently.

The next way we encourage each other is by praising abundantly.

- The Greek word for *encouragement* that we discussed earlier, *parakaleo*, is used 110 times in the New Testament. What does the frequency of this word indicate about the instruction to praise one another?
- How do you feel when you receive words of encouragement? Do you relish the experience, or does it make you uncomfortable? Why do you think you react that way?
- How do you feel about Max's suggestion to call a friend simply to encourage him or her? Would this come naturally for you? How would you feel if someone did this to you?

8. Max shared a story about a man in his congregation, Charles Prince, who encouraged him in his ministry.
   - How did Charles's encouragement affect Max?
   - Do you currently have a Charles Prince in your life? If so, who is it, and how does that person encourage you?
   - Did you have a Charles Prince in the past? How did that person encourage you?

9. Pick one person you will encourage this week in a way that calls forth the Rocky within.

- How will you encourage that person? By listening intently? By praising abundantly?
- Note how you feel afterward. Did making someone else happy through biblical encouragement make you happy as well?

3

Don't Pet the Peeves

1. What are some of your biggest pet peeves, and why? Have these been pet peeves for a long time, or can you trace them back to a more recent point?

2. The person who suffers from a pet peeve is not the one with the irritating behavior but the one who is annoyed by it. Has your pet peeve ever stolen your joy? If so, describe what happened.

3. How would you define the word *patience*?

4. Do you consider yourself a patient person?
   - In what situations is it difficult for you to be patient? Why?
   - In what situations is it easier for you to be patient? Why?

5. According to Ephesians 4:1–3, how did Paul say to respond in all situations?

6. By looking at other translations and considering the context of this passage, we can learn more about the biblical idea of patience. The New King James Version, Ephesians 4:1–3 says, "I, therefore, the prisoner of the Lord, beseech you to walk worthy of the calling

with which you were called, with all lowliness and gentleness, with longsuffering, bearing with one another in love, endeavoring to keep the unity of the Spirit in the bond of peace."

- What word is used here in place of *patience*?
- How does this translation help you understand the meaning and purpose of patience?
- Paul referred to himself as "the prisoner of the Lord," which was not only metaphorical but literal. Paul spent time in prison during his ministry, and the last two years of his life were spent under house arrest in Rome. Why do you think he reminded his audience of this when talking about patience and longsuffering?
- Longsuffering is listed as one of the characteristics of those who are worthy of the calling as Christ followers. How does longsuffering make us worthy of this calling?
- In the Gospels how do we see Jesus exhibiting patience and longsuffering?

7. Now consider the Phillips translation of Ephesians 4:2: "Accept life with humility and patience, making allowances for each other."
   - How could patience and humility be related?
   - How does patience help us make allowances for each other?
   - Think about what it is like for others to live with you or be in a relationship with you. What are some of your weaknesses or characteristics that might get on other people's nerves?
   - Describe a time that someone made an allowance for you when you were being difficult. How did that person show you patience? How did it make you feel about that person?

8. Read Matthew 7:3–5.
   - What did Jesus say to do before pointing out the speck of dust in your friend's eye?
   - Which is more typical of you, removing the big piece of wood from your own eye or noticing the speck of dust in your friend's eye? Why?

9. Max says, "Look at yourself before you look down on others. Rather than put them in their place, put yourself in their place" (p. 36).
   - Think of someone who annoys you, someone who has a speck of dust in his or her eye and you desperately want to point it out. How could you put yourself in that person's shoes?
   - Does empathizing with this person change the way you feel about the dust in his or her eye?

10. Are there any pet peeves you used to have that no longer bother you? If so, what were they, and how did you overcome them?

11. At the end of this chapter, Max describes the trees along the Guadalupe River. He says they are bent, not straight, and yet they provide a haven for people and animals and birds.
    - How does he compare us to those trees? What do you think of this metaphor?
    - What is one pet peeve, annoyance, or behavior that tends to test your patience?
    - How could you start to see this "bentness" as a beautiful part of God's creation rather than an irritation?

4

The Sweet Sound of
a Second Fiddle

1. Read the story of Mary and Martha in Luke 10:38–42. On first read which character in the story do you identify with most: Mary, who is sitting at Jesus' feet; Martha, who is preparing dinner; or Jesus himself, who is enjoying talking to Mary and the others who have gathered? Explain your answer.

2. Now reread Max's reimagining of this passage on pages 46–49.
   - After reading this did you identify with any other characters?
   - If so, which ones, and why?

3. Max says Martha's downfall was not her work or her request that Mary help her; it was her motivation. According to Max, what was Martha's likely motivation?

4. When do you feel tempted to perform? At church, at work, with friends, with your family? What sort of recognition do you crave in these situations?

5. Do you agree that social media has affected our desire for approval and applause?

- How has social media affected you in this area?
- In general how do you feel about yourself after scrolling through social media?
- Would you say social media makes you more or less happy? Why?

6. Why is approval from others not a good indicator of happiness?
   - Whose approval do you want most right now, and why?
   - What amount or type of approval from this person would it take to make you happy?
   - How would you feel if you never received this person's approval?

7. Just as we perform for others to gain their applause, we often perform for God as well.
   - What are some ways you work for God's approval?
   - Are there any activities or spiritual practices you engage in that are motivated more by a desire for approval than a desire to grow in intimacy with God?

8. How do you react to the statement that we are not God's VIP or MVP?
   - Does this idea bother you or confuse you? Do you agree or disagree? Why?
   - If we are not God's VIP or MVP, what are we to him?

9. The Corinthian church made the mistake of considering Paul and Apollos, his fellow worker in Christ, as more important than God. To this, Paul said, "Is Apollos important? No! Is Paul important? No! We are only servants of God who helped you believe. Each

one of us did the work God gave us to do. I planted the seed, and Apollos watered it. But God is the One who made it grow. So the one who plants is not important, and the one who waters is not important. Only God, who makes things grow, is important" (1 Cor. 3:5–7 NCV).

- According to this passage who is important?
- Who is not important?
- Do you resist accepting what Paul said here, or does it resonate with you? Explain your response.

10. Consider the following passages:

"Look at the birds of the air, for they neither sow nor reap nor gather into barns; yet your heavenly Father feeds them. Are you not of more value than they?" (Matt. 6:26).

"For You formed my inward parts;
You covered me in my mother's womb.
I will praise You, for I am fearfully and wonderfully made;
Marvelous are Your works,
And that my soul knows very well" (Ps. 139:13–14).

"For God so loved the world that He gave His only begotten Son, that whoever believes in Him should not perish but have everlasting life. For God did not send His Son into the world to condemn the world, but that the world through Him might be saved" (John 3:16–17).

These verses indicate a God who cares deeply for us as his children.

- How do we reconcile the tension of not being important, as Paul described in 1 Corinthians 3:5–8, with also being God's beloved child?

- According to these passages what makes us important to God?
- How is this different from being praised or applauded by God for our good works?
- How could being confident in God's love actually help us consider others more important than ourselves?

11. Romans 12:15 says, "Rejoice with those who rejoice" (NIV). Max says this is a good way to take the focus off ourselves. He suggests putting this verse into practice by setting a goal to celebrate everything good that happens to someone else for the next twenty-four hours.
    - Are you willing to accept this challenge?
    - How will you celebrate in a genuine way the good things you see happening to others?
    - Record how this experiment affects your happiness level.

5

The Fine Art of
Saying "Hello"

1. At the beginning of this chapter, Max describes a CEO who has decided to take a leave of absence from his company.
   - What reason did the CEO state for doing this?
   - What were his employees lacking?

2. Have you ever been in a work or home environment like the one Max describes?
   - Were you the victim of disrespect, or did you disrespect someone else?
   - Why do you think that environment encouraged disrespect?

3. In his letters Paul often instructed the church to greet each other with a kiss. Consider the following verses:

   "Greet one another with a holy kiss" (Rom. 16:16).

   "Give each other a holy kiss when you meet" (1 Cor. 16:20 NCV).

   "Greet each other with a holy kiss" (2 Cor. 13:12 NCV).

   "Give each other a holy kiss when you meet" (1 Thess. 5:26 NCV).

   "Greet one another with a kiss of love" (1 Peter 5:14).

Have you ever paid much attention to this instruction from Paul? Why or why not?

4. In the culture of the day, this type of greeting was reserved for close friends, family members, and those who were objects of respect.
   - How do you greet your family members, close friends, and people you respect?
   - Is it different from the way you greet other people? If so, why do you greet them differently?

5. Paul's letter to the Roman church addressed serious issues within the community as well as deep theological questions. Because of this it might seem odd that Paul took the time to include the instruction to greet one another with a holy kiss (Rom. 16:16). Why do you think Paul included this in his letter?

6. Give an example of what you think respect for others looks like.
   - What about this scenario exhibits respect?
   - Why is respecting one another important?

7. Showing respect for others is easy when you truly respect them, but how do you treat a person with respect if you don't actually respect that person? Do you think we are called to respect everyone? Why or why not?

8. We see examples of greeting others with a holy kiss as early as Genesis 33 when the brothers Jacob and Esau reunited. Jacob and Esau had a strained history. Jacob had tricked their father, Isaac, into blessing him rather than Esau, who as the firstborn should

have been blessed. Esau was so angry he wanted to kill Jacob, but Jacob ran away (Gen. 27). The brothers spent the next several years estranged.

When they finally saw each other again, Esau clearly had experienced a change of heart. Scripture says, "Esau ran to meet [Jacob], and embraced him, and fell on his neck and kissed him, and they wept" (Gen. 33:4).

Esau not only greeted his brother with a kiss—a sign of respect—but he also "embraced" him and "fell on his neck." Read Genesis 33:1–16.

- How did Jacob respond to Esau's show of love, respect, and affection?
- Why do you think Esau was able to show respect for Jacob even after Jacob had disrespected him?
- How can this story encourage you to respect someone who is difficult to respect?
- How will you greet that person the next time you see him or her? What can you do to ensure you treat all people equally?

9. In the story about the recently released convict and the mayor, how did the mayor greet the convict?
   - How did his greeting affect the convict?
   - Has anyone ever unexpectedly treated you with respect? If so, how did it affect you?

10. Read Romans 16:1–16.
    - What is unique about this list of people Paul greeted?
    - What does this list tell us about whom we should greet?

11. Think about your day yesterday.
    - Where did you go?
    - Whom did you talk to?
    - Did you overlook greeting someone at work or in a store or even in your own home? Why didn't you greet that person?

12. Now, think about your day ahead.
    - How could you go out of your way to greet someone you typically don't greet?
    - How might this add to that person's happiness—and to yours?

6

The Power Posture

1. Intercessory prayer is the act of praying on another person's behalf.
   - Is this type of prayer a part of your daily life? Why or why not?
   - Do you believe intercessory prayer can be beneficial? Why or why not?
   - Have you ever prayed for someone and the prayer was answered the way you wanted it to be? If so, how did that experience affect you?
   - Have you ever prayed for someone and the prayer was not answered the way you wanted it to be? If so, how did that experience affect you?

2. Read Genesis 18:16–33.
   - How would you characterize Abraham in this passage? Bold? Crazy? Audacious? Naive?
   - Why did Abraham bargain with God to save Sodom?

3. Genesis 18:16–33 is the first recorded instance in Scripture of a human asking God to reconsider his plans.
   - How did God respond to Abraham's pleas?
   - What does this tell you about God?
   - What does this tell you about the power of praying for one another?

4. Perhaps it's easier to believe God would listen to someone like Abraham, the father of the Israelite nation, than to believe God would listen to us. Do you ever struggle to believe that God listens to your prayers? Why or why not?

5. Read Matthew 8:5–13.
   - Why did Jesus heal the servant of the centurion?
   - How does Jesus' response to the centurion mirror God's response to Abraham?
   - What does this story reveal about the relationship God wants with us through Christ?

6. Scripture says that in Christ, we are God's children (1 John 3:1), ambassadors for Christ (2 Cor. 5:20), and a part of the holy priesthood (1 Peter 2:5). How do these descriptions affect the way you view the power of your prayers?

7. Fill in the blank: "When we pray for one another, we enter God's workshop, pick up a hammer, and _____ him to accomplish his purpose."
   - What do you think about the idea of your prayers helping God accomplish his purpose?
   - How do you reconcile this with the fact that God is all-powerful and all-knowing? See Jeremiah 32:17 and Isaiah 46:9–10.

8. Consider the following verses in James:
   "Come near to God, and God will come near to you" (4:8 NCV).

   "When a believing person prays, great things happen" (5:16 NCV).

James's letter was written to a community of Jewish Christians during a time of great oppression. The Roman Empire had taken the land of those who lived in rural areas in Palestine, forcing them to work the land of wealthy aristocrats who did not treat them fairly.[2] The Christians probably felt powerless as a minority governed by another authority. We know they were suffering because James opened his letter with "My brethren, count it all joy when you fall into various trials" (1:2).

- Knowing this about James's audience, why do you think he instructed them to pray?
- Is there a situation in your life in which you feel powerless?
- If so, have you prayed about it? Why or why not?

9. Max cites a study conducted by Dr. Harold G. Koenig at Duke University that found people who pray or ask for divine assistance "cope with stress better, they experience greater well-being because they have more hope, they're more optimistic, they experience less depression, less anxiety, and they commit suicide less often" (p. 80).

- What do you think about this study's findings?
- Has this been the effect of prayer in your life? What is your answer based on?

10. How can intercessory prayer activate happiness in your own life? Have you ever experienced this after praying for someone else? If so, describe that experience.

11. Return to your answers in the first question.
- What new thoughts about the role of intercessory prayer has this chapter prompted?

- If the idea of praying for someone else is still difficult for you, why do think that is true? Do you feel powerless in the face of that person's circumstances? Do you not trust that God will listen to you? Do you not believe you are worth listening to?
- Spend some time thinking about what stops you from praying for others more often.

12. Think about someone in your life who could use your prayers. How could you place yourself between that person in need and the One who can meet that need?

7

It's Your Serve

1. Max opens this chapter with a story about his Sunday school teacher who helped lead him to Christ. Max describes the teacher as a "quiet servant."
   - Have you ever encountered a quiet servant like this?
   - If so, who was that person? How did he or she impact you?

2. How are quiet servants viewed in your community and culture?
   - Are they valued or overlooked?
   - How does this attitude toward quiet servants affect your desire to serve others?

3. In Galatians 5:13 Paul said, "For you, brethren, have been called to liberty; only do not use liberty as an opportunity for the flesh, but through love serve one another." The Greek word translated as *serve* in this passage is *douleuó*, which suggests serving as someone who is in bondage and must obey and submit to another person's authority. A few verses before this in Galatians 4:7, Paul declared to his readers that they were no longer slaves but were children of God.
   - If Paul said the Galatians were no longer slaves but children of God, why did he call them to serve as if they were in bondage?

- How can our freedom increase our desire to serve one another?
- Have you experienced this in the Christian life? If so, how?

4. Christ entered the world through the person of Mary. Have you paid much attention to what Scripture says about her? Why or why not?

5. Read Luke 1:26–38.
   - What do these verses tell you about the type of person Mary was?
   - What do these verses tell you about the type of person God uses to accomplish his will and his purpose?
   - Why do you think God uses quiet servants?

6. Jesus exemplified servanthood in his life, death, and resurrected body. Read the following passages: Matthew 9:35–36, Mark 8:1–10, Luke 23:44–49, John 21:4–14.
   - How did Jesus serve?
   - Whom did Jesus serve?
   - Which of these examples of servitude resonates with you most, and why?

7. Jesus was the perfect example of a servant. He even said that he did not come to earth to be served but to serve (Matt. 20:28). But those of us who are active in a church community and in our faith can still find it difficult to serve one another. Why is that?
   - What opportunity do you have to serve others?
   - If you're not currently taking advantage of that opportunity, what keeps you from doing so?

8. Describe a recent time that you served someone else.
   - How did you serve that person?
   - How did that person react?
   - How did serving him or her make you feel?

9. Psychologist Bernard Rimland conducted a study that linked unselfishness with happiness.
   - Why do you think unselfish people are happier?
   - Have you observed your happiness level being affected by your selfishness level? If so, how?

10. Sometimes we don't serve because we think we don't have the time or the energy. Read Isaiah 58:10–11.
    - What does this passage say will happen if you give yourself to the hungry and satisfy the needs of the afflicted?
    - How could these verses encourage you to serve even if you feel low on time or strength?
    - Have you ever experienced God's help or strength when you were serving someone even though you didn't believe you had the resources to do so?
    - How did God help you?
    - What did that experience teach you about the role service plays in the Christian life?

11. For some the problem is not that they don't serve enough but that they serve too much. Jesus exemplified being a servant, but he also exemplified taking rest. Read Luke 5:15–16.
    - During Jesus' ministry how did he balance serving multitudes of people with taking time for rest?

- What are some examples of Jesus resting? How did he spend those times?
- How could you incorporate into your busy schedule of serving others Jesus' habit of resting and retreating?

12. Identify where your heart is today in the area of serving.
    - Do you resist it? Why? What is stopping you? How could you invite the Holy Spirit to help you serve others?
    - Or do you serve so much that you feel you're on the brink of burnout? What area of service could you step back from for at least a season? What specific type of rest would you incorporate?

8

Discomfort Zones

1. Have you ever been in a situation where you did not feel accepted because of who you were? If so, describe that situation.
   - How did you handle that situation?
   - What helped you work through it?
   - Have you witnessed someone else not being accepted? Explain.
   - How did this experience alter the way you treat others?

2. In Luke 5:1–11 Jesus calls Peter, James, and John—three fishermen from the region of Galilee—to be his disciples. A few verses later, in Luke 5:27–28, Jesus calls Levi (also known as Matthew) to be his disciple as well.
   - How was Levi different from Peter, James, and John?
   - What does this say about who Jesus is and those he wants to follow him?

3. In Luke 5:29–31 Levi throws a banquet for Jesus and invites his (Levi's) friends.
   - What kind of people are at the banquet?
   - What did the Pharisees think of this party and the guests in attendance?
   - What is Jesus' response to the Pharisees?

4. Read Luke 5:29–31 three more times. Each time put yourself in the shoes of one of the characters in the story: Levi, the tax collectors and sinners, and the Pharisees.

   • What do you think it was like to be Levi at this banquet after he had met Jesus? Do you identify with anything about him and his story? If so, what?

   • What do you think it was like to be a tax collector or a sinner sharing a table with Jesus? Do you identify with anything about this group of people? If so, what?

   • What do you think it was like to be a Pharisee witnessing this scene? Do you identify with the Pharisees' response and behavior? If so, how?

5. Max says, "Your Levi is your 'opposite you.'" Identify a Levi in your life.

   • What makes that person your "opposite you"?

   • What is it like to interact with him or her?

6. In Romans 15:7 Paul wrote, "Accept one another, then, just as Christ accepted you, in order to bring praise to God" (NIV). Why do we accept one another?

7. The Greek word translated as *accept* in Romans 15:7 is *proslambanó*, which means "to welcome into one's fellowship and into one's heart."

   • What does this definition tell you about how Christians are to accept one another?

   • Have you accepted your Levi in this way? Why or why not?

8. Accepting one another can be confusing when you might fundamentally disagree with the behavior or beliefs of the other person.
   - Do you think we are called to accept everyone no matter what? Why or why not?
   - What is the difference between accepting someone and endorsing that person's behavior?

9. In John 14:3 Jesus said to his disciples, "And if I go and prepare a place for you, I will come again and receive you to Myself; that where I am, there you may be also." The word Jesus used for "receive" is *proslambanó*, the same word Paul used in Romans 15:7. What does this tell you about how Jesus accepts us?

10. Max points out that Jesus was filled with grace and also with truth (John 1:14).
    - What do the words *grace* and *truth* mean to you?
    - How did Jesus show grace and truth in the way he treated the woman who was caught in adultery? (See John 8:2–11.)
    - Balancing grace and truth is tricky. When working to accept others, do you tend to lean more toward grace or truth? Why?

11. Read Romans 15:7 again.
    - What does accepting one another do for God?
    - How is God praised when we accept each other?
    - How could this motivate you as you work toward accepting others?

12. Practicing empathy, as you did when you read Luke 5:29–31 with three different perspectives, can go a long way in accepting one

another. Max quotes Raleigh Washington, an African American minister who's devoted much of his life to racial reconciliation, as saying the most important statement he makes when trying to bridge racial divides is "Help me understand what it's like to be you."

- Have you ever considered what it's like to be your Levi?
- Could you ask your Levi to tell you what it is like to be him or her?
- How would understanding your Levi help you accept your Levi?

9

Speak Up

1. How do you respond when you are "invited into someone's hurt" (p. 121)?
   - Do you encourage that person with words? Listen to him or her? Serve him or her?
   - Why is this your go-to response?
   - When you're in pain, how do you want people to respond to you?

2. Has anyone ever shared his or her pain with you but also expressed disbelief that God would bring relief to that pain? If so, how did you respond?
   - Have you ever told someone you were in pain and didn't believe God would help you?
   - If so, how did that person respond?
   - Was it helpful? Explain why or why not.

3. When Jesus arrived four days after Lazarus's death, Martha said, "Lord, if only you had been here, my brother would not have died" (John 11:21 NLT). How did Jesus respond to Martha in John 11:25–26?

4. The Greek word translated as *admonish* is *noutheteó*,[3] which means to exhort. An exhortation is an encouragement with a

calling. Consider the following verses. The words in bold are all translations of *noutheteó*:

Colossians 1:28: "Him we preach, **warning** every man and teaching every man in all wisdom, that we may present every man perfect in Christ Jesus."

Colossians 3:16: "Let the word of Christ dwell in you richly in all wisdom, teaching and **admonishing** one another in psalms and hymns and spiritual songs, singing with grace in your hearts to the Lord."

1 Corinthians 4:14–16: "I do not write these things to shame you, but as my beloved children I **warn** you. For though you might have ten thousand instructors in Christ, yet you do not have many fathers; for in Christ Jesus I have begotten you through the gospel. Therefore I urge you, imitate me."

- What insights into the purpose of admonition do these verses provide?
- How is admonishing different from simply encouraging?
- Have you ever been admonished by someone?
- What did that person say, and how did it make you feel?

5. Before Jesus went to Bethlehem to visit Mary and Martha following Lazarus's death, what did he tell his disciples? (See John 11:4.)
   - What did Jesus say was the purpose of Lazarus's death?
   - Consequently, why could Jesus admonish Martha the way he did (John 11:25–26) even before he raised Lazarus back to life?

6. Have you had a tragedy in your life that you now see was, as Jesus said, "for the glory of God"?

- What was the event, and how did it glorify God?
- Has this experience helped you admonish others when they were facing a tragic circumstance? If so, how?

7. It's easy to admonish others when our faith is strong, but how can we admonish others when our faith is weak?
   - Have you ever tried to encourage someone in his or her faith when you weren't sure about your own? What did you say?
   - Hebrews 4:12–13 says, "His powerful Word is sharp as a surgeon's scalpel, cutting through everything, whether doubt or defense, laying us open to listen and obey. Nothing and no one is impervious to God's Word. We can't get away from it—no matter what" (THE MESSAGE). Who can get away from God's Word?
   - How can you use God's Word to admonish yourself?
   - Do you have any go-to passages like Max lists in this chapter? If so, what are they? If not, write down a few verses that you find encouraging.

8. What does Max say is the job of the church?
   - Have members of your faith community ever helped lead you back to your faith? How did they do this for you?
   - Do you know anyone who needs help getting back on the path of faith? If so, who? How could you admonish that person this week?

10

You've Been Bustered

1. What do you think about the phrase "forgive and forget"?
   - Is this a life motto for you?
   - Do you believe it's possible?
   - Have you successfully practiced this in your life?
   - Explain your answers.

2. According to this chapter what does forgiveness *not* do? Do you agree? Why or why not?

3. What is forgiveness, as described by Max? Is this how you've viewed forgiveness in the past, or does this differ from your definition of forgiveness? If so, how?

4. From your experience how do you know when you've truly forgiven a person? How do you know when you haven't forgiven someone?

5. Think about a time you were able to forgive someone who hurt you. What made you able to forgive that person?

6. According to a study done at Duke University, four of the eight factors that promote emotional stability are related to forgiveness:

Avoiding suspicion and resentment

Not living in the past

Not wasting time and energy fighting conditions that can't be changed

Refusing to indulge in self-pity when handed a raw deal

- Which of these factors do you struggle with, and why?
- Which of these would you say you do well, and why?

7. In Ephesians 4:32 Paul wrote, "Be kind to one another, tenderhearted, forgiving one another, even as God in Christ forgave you."
   - Have you experienced Christ's forgiveness in your life?
   - If so, has this affected how and why you forgive others?
   - If not, how does the idea of Christ's forgiveness of your sin make you feel? Is that easy or difficult to accept? Explain your answer.

8. Read Max's reimagining of John 13:3–5 on pages 138–139. Read it slowly. Imagine yourself as one of the characters in the scene.
   - What details in this passage stuck out to you, and why?
   - What does this passage teach us about Jesus?

9. Read John 18:2–5, 15–17. Jesus washed Peter's and Judas's feet, knowing they would betray him.
   - What does this tell you about the nature of Christ's forgiveness?
   - What does this tell you about how Christ has forgiven you?
   - What does this tell you about Christ's forgiveness for the people in your life who have been difficult for you to forgive?

---

10. What was Jesus' instruction to the disciples right after he washed their feet? (See John 13:14–15.)

    - Considering this passage, think about a person you know you need to forgive but haven't yet.
    - What is your motivation for forgiving this person?
    - How could awareness of the forgiveness you've received help you forgive this person?

11. With this same person in mind, think through the steps toward forgiveness that Max suggests in this chapter:

    Decide what you need to forgive.

    Ask yourself why it hurts.

    Take it to Jesus.

    Tell your offender.

    Pray for your offender.

    Conduct a funeral.

    - Which of these steps have you already taken?
    - Which do you still need to take? What's stopping you?
    - How could fully forgiving this person add to your happiness?
    - How is not forgiving this person stealing from your happiness?

12. The book of Ephesians was originally a letter Paul wrote to a church community. This suggests that his instructions to forgive pertain not only to individuals but also to the church as a body.

    - What must this community have been going through for Paul to give these instructions in Ephesians 4:32?
    - How can forgiveness affect an entire community?
    - How can withholding forgiveness affect an entire community?
    - How can being a part of a community help us forgive one another?

11

Be Loved, Then Love

1. Max opens this chapter with a story about Andrea Mosconi. What was Mosconi tasked with? How are we tasked in a similar way?

2. Who is someone who brings out the best in you, and how do they do that?

3. Perhaps the greatest command Jesus ever gave is recorded in John 13:34 when he said, "A new commandment I give to you, that you love one another; as I have loved you." This command is repeated later in the New Testament. Consider the following passages along with John 13:34:

   Romans 13:8: "Owe no one anything except to love one another, for he who loves another has fulfilled the law."

   1 John 4:11: "Beloved, if God so loved us, we also ought to love one another."
   - What do these verses say about how and why we are to love one another?
   - In your own words describe what it means and what it looks like to love another person.

- The Greek word translated as *love* in all three of these verses is *agape*. What does *agape* mean?
- How does this word help define what Jesus meant when he said we ought to love one another?

4. Max poses an important question in this chapter on page 153: "Have you let God love you?"
   - What is your answer to that question?
   - If it's yes, how do you feel God's love?
   - If it's no, explain your answer.
   - If you're uncertain, describe what you're uncertain about.

5. We can't fully love others until we accept the love of Christ. When we experience the love of the Savior, we can love others.
   - Has accepting God's love helped you love other people? If so, how?
   - Have you ever tried to love someone when you didn't feel loved? What was that experience like?

6. Read the following verses: Deuteronomy 7:7–9; Romans 5:8; Ephesians 2:8–10.
   - According to these passages why does God love us?
   - Why did Jesus die for us?
   - Do you believe God loves you simply because he chose you? Or do you find yourself working to earn the approval and favor of other people and God?
   - Can you think of a person you know who lives as if he or she is loved by God? What indicates that this person feels loved?

7. Think of a person or a group of people who are difficult for you to love.

   - How could God's love for you help you love this person or group of people?
   - How would loving this person or group of people cause happiness to happen in you?

8. In his book *Life of the Beloved*, Henri Nouwen writes about how difficult it is for us to believe we are loved by God. In order to help us with this, Nouwen suggests making a practice of sitting in silence and listening for the voice of God.

   "It is not easy to enter into the silence and reach beyond the many boisterous and demanding voices of our world," Nouwen writes. But if you do, he says, you will not encounter a berating voice that is punishing you or displeased with you. Instead, you will "discover there the small intimate voice saying: 'You are my Beloved Child, on you my favor rests' . . . if we dare to embrace our solitude and befriend our silence, we will come to know that voice."[4]

   - What do you think God would tell you if you spent time being silent in his presence?
   - Is this an uncomfortable thought for you? Why or why not?
   - Could you trust what Nouwen says here and believe that God would call you his Beloved Child?
   - Spend some time in silence today and listen for the voice of God, who is simply saying, "I love you."

The Next Step

The Happiness Challenge

1. Max set the challenge to make one hundred people happy over the next forty days.
   - Are you willing to commit to this?
   - Does anything about this challenge make you hesitant? If so, what?
   - Does anything about this challenge excite you? If so, what?

2. Throughout this book you learned ten different ways to make others happy and, therefore, yourself happy:

   Encourage one another (1 Thess. 5:11).
   Bear with one another (Eph. 4:2).
   Regard one another as more important (Phil. 2:4).
   Greet one another (Rom. 16:16).
   Pray for one another (James 5:16).
   Serve one another (Gal. 5:13).
   Accept one another (Rom. 15:7).
   Admonish one another (Col. 3:16).
   Forgive one another (Eph. 4:32).
   Love one another (1 John 3:11).
   - Name two or three of these you feel comfortable pursuing during the next forty days to make others happy.

———

- Name two or three of these that are more challenging for you but that you are willing to attempt during the next forty days.

3. Assess your happiness level right now. On a scale of one to ten, how happy would you say you are ?

4. Spend a few minutes thinking about five people whose happiness you want to increase over the next forty days. Write down their names and how you could bring some happiness into their lives using a "one another" passage.

5. After you've completed the forty-day challenge, consider the following questions:

   - How would you measure your current happiness level compared to what it was before this challenge?

   - What was the most memorable part of this challenge for you, and why?

   - What was difficult about this challenge, and why?

   - How could you make this happiness a part of your everyday life?

Notes

Chapter 1: The Unexpected Door to Joy

1. "Mr. Happy Man—Johnny Barnes," YouTube, https://www.youtube.com /watch?v=v_EX5NzqNXc. See also Jarrod Stackelroth, "Mr. Happy Man," *Adventist Record*, July 21, 2016, https://record.adventistchurch.com/2016 /07/21/mr-happy-man/.

2. Kathy Caprino, "The Top 10 Things People Want in Life but Can't Seem to Get," Huffington Post, updated December 6, 2017, https://www .huffingtonpost.com/kathy-caprino/the-top-10-things-people-_2_b _9564982.html.

3. David Shimer, "Yale's Most Popular Class Ever: Happiness," *New York Times*, January 26, 2018, https://www.nytimes.com/2018/01/26/nyregion /at-yale-class-on-happiness-draws-huge-crowd-laurie-santos.html.

4. Sonja Lyubomirsky, *The How of Happiness: A Practical Approach to Getting the Life You Want* (London: Piatkus, 2007), 25.

5. Ed Diener, Carol Nickerson, Richard E. Lucas, Ed Sandvik, "Dispositional Affect and Job Outcomes," *Social Indicators Research* 59, no. 3 (September 2002): 229–59, https://link.springer.com/article/10.1023/A:1019672513984.

6. Shana Lebowitz, "A New Study Finds a Key Component of Effective

Leadership Is Surprisingly Simple," *Business Insider*, August 19, 2015, http://www.businessinsider.com/why-happy-people-are-better-leaders-2015-8.

7. Alexandra Sifferlin, "Here's How Happy Americans Are Right Now," *Time*, July 26, 2017, http://time.com/4871720/how-happy-are-americans/.

8. Lyubomirsky, *The How of Happiness*, 37.

9. Pamela Cowan, "Depression Will Be the Second Leading Cause of Disease by 2020: WHO," *Calgary Herald*, October 7, 2010, http://www.calgaryherald.com/health/Depression+will+second+leading+cause+disease+2020/3640325/story.html.

10. Jean M. Twenge, "Why Adults Are Less Happy Than They Used to Be: But Young People Are Happier," *Psychology Today*, November 6, 2015, https://www.psychologytoday.com/blog/our-changing-culture/201511/why-adults-are-less-happy-they-used-be.

11. Lyubomirsky, *The How of Happiness*, 20–21.

12. Melissa Dahl, "A Classic Psychology Study on Why Winning the Lottery Won't Make You Happier," *The Cut*, January 13, 2016, https://www.thecut.com/2016/01/classic-study-on-happiness-and-the-lottery.html.

13. Daniel Kahneman and Angus Deaton, "High Income Improves Evaluation of Life but Not Emotional Well-Being," PNAS, August 4, 2010, p. 3, http://www.pnas.org/content/early/2010/08/27/1011492107.

14. Ed Diener, Jeff Horwitz, and Robert A. Emmons, "Happiness of the Very Wealthy," Social Indicators Research 16, 263–74, https://emmons.faculty.ucdavis.edu/wp-content/uploads/sites/90/2015/08/1985_1happiness-wealthy.pdf.

15. Carey Goldberg, quoting Daniel Gilbert, "Too Much of a Good Thing," *Boston Globe*, February 6, 2006, http://archive.boston.com/yourlife/health/mental/articles/2006/02/06/too_much_of_a_good_thing/.

16. Berkeley Wellness, "What Is the Science of Happiness?" November 9, 2015, http://www.berkeleywellness.com/healthy-mind/mind-body/article/what-science-happiness.

17. Lyubomirsky, *The How of Happiness*, 23.

18. Randy Alcorn, *Happiness* (Carol Stream, IL: Tyndale, 2015), 19.

Chapter 2: Gimme Five, Rocky

1. W. E. Vine, *Vine's Expository Dictionary of New Testament Words: A Comprehensive Dictionary of the Original Greek Words with Their Precise*

Meanings for English Readers (McLean, VA: MacDonald Publishing, n.d.), "Comfort, Comforter, Comfortless," 209–10.

2. Vine, *Vine's Expository Dictionary*, "Encourage, Encouragement," 366.

3. Hara Estroff Marano, "Marriage Math," *Psychology Today*, March 16, 2004, https://www.psychologytoday.com/us/articles/200403/marriage-math.

4. Jack Zenger and Joseph Folkman, "The Ideal Praise-to-Criticism Ratio," *Harvard Business Review*, March 15, 2013, https://hbr.org/2013/03/the -ideal-praise-to-criticism.

5. Lynne Malcolm, "Scientific Evidence Points to Importance of Positive Thinking," ABC RN, June 17, 2015, http://www.abc.net.au/radionational /programs/allinthemind/the-scientific-evidence-for-positive-thinking /6553614.

6. Quoted in Alan Loy McGinnis, *The Friendship Factor: How to Get Closer to the People You Care For* (Minneapolis: Augsburg, 1979), 69.

7. Andrew Shain, "As He Heads to the U.S. Senate, Tim Scott Praises Early Mentor," *Beaufort Gazette*, July 2, 2013, http://www.islandpacket.com/news /local/community/beaufort-news/article33492450.html.

8. Vine, *Vine's Expository Dictionary*, "Consider," 231–32.

9. Gary Smalley and John Trent, *Leaving the Light On: Building the Memories That Will Draw Your Kids Home* (Sisters, OR: Multnomah, 1994), 27–28.

10. McGinnis, *The Friendship Factor*, 95.

Chapter 3: Don't Pet the Peeves

1. W. E. Vine, *Vine's Expository Dictionary of New Testament Words: A Comprehensive Dictionary of the Original Greek Words with Their Precise Meanings for English Readers* (McLean, VA: MacDonald Publishing, n.d.), "Longsuffering," 694.

2. David Hocking, "The Patience of God," Blue Letter Bible, https://www .blueletterbible.org/comm/hocking_david/attributes/attributes14.cfm.

3. Quoted in Alan Loy McGinnis, *The Friendship Factor: How to Get Closer to the People You Care For* (Minneapolis: Augsburg, 1979), 69.

4. Story contributed by Alice H. Cook, *Reader's Digest*, December 1996, 140.

Chapter 4: The Sweet Sound of a Second Fiddle

1. Hannah Whitall Smith, *The Christian's Secret of a Holy Life: The Unpublished Personal Writings of Hannah Whitall Smith*, ed. Melvin E. Dieter (Grand Rapids: Zondervan, 1994), 10–11.

Chapter 5: The Fine Art of Saying "Hello"

1. Deborah Norville, *The Power of Respect: Benefit from the Most Forgotten Element of Success* (Nashville: Thomas Nelson, 2009), 6–8.
2. John Henry Jowett, *The Best of John Henry Jowett*, ed. Gerald Kennedy (New York: Harper and Brothers, 1948), 89, https://archive.org/stream /bestofjohnhenryj012480mbp/bestofjohnhenryj012480mbp_djvu.txt).
3. Sonja Lyubomirsky, *The How of Happiness: A Practical Approach to Getting the Life You Want* (London: Piatkus, 2007), 150–51.
4. Kasley Killam, "A Hug a Day Keeps the Doctor Away," *Scientific American*, March 17, 2015, https://www.scientificamerican.com/article/a-hug-a-day -keeps-the-doctor-away/.
5. John Stott, *Romans: God's Good News for the World* (Downers Grove, IL: InterVarsity, 1994), 395.
6. "Aristobulus," Bible Hub, http://biblehub.com/topical/a/aristobulus.htm.
7. E. Badian, "Narcissus: Roman Official," *Encyclopaedia Britannica*, http:// www.britannica.com/biography/narcissus-roman-official.
8. This is believed because Mark, whose gospel was written in or for Rome, is the only Evangelist who mentions the names of Simon's sons and does so in a way as to imply they were already known. See Mark 15:21.
9. "Sumter County Church Chronology," June 1965 entry, http://www .sumtercountyhistory.com/church/SC_ChurchChr.htm.

Chapter 6: The Power Posture

1. "Science Proves the Healing Power of Prayer," NewsmaxHealth, March 31, 2015, https://www.newsmax.com/health/headline/prayer-health-faith -medicine/2015/03/31/id/635623/.
2. Eben Alexander, *Proof of Heaven: A Neurosurgeon's Journey into the Afterlife* (New York: Simon and Schuster, 2012), 38, 45–46, 103.
3. Dan Pratt, *Tears on the Church House Floor* (Bloomington, IN: WestBow, 2018), 74–76.

Chapter 7: It's Your Serve

1. "The United Healthcare/Volunteer Match Do Good Live Well Study," March 2010: 19, 33, 43, https://cdn.volunteermatch.org/www/about /UnitedHealthcare_VolunteerMatch_Do_Good_Live_Well_Study.pdf.
2. Bernard Rimland, "The Altruism Paradox," *Psychological Reports* 51, no. 2 (October 1982): 521–2, http://www.amscie.pub.com/doi/abs/10.2466

/pr0.1982.51.2.521, quoted in Randy Alcorn, *Happiness* (Carol Stream, IL: Tyndale, 2015), 291.

Chapter 8: Discomfort Zones

1. W. E. Vine, *Vine's Expository Dictionary of New Testament Words: A Comprehensive Dictionary of the Original Greek Words with Their Precise Meanings for English Readers* (McLean, VA: MacDonald Publishing, n.d.), "Pharisees," 863.
2. John Stott, *Romans: God's Good News for the World* (Downers Grove, IL: InterVarsity, 1994), 359.
3. Told to me in person and used by permission.
4. Quoted in Alan Loy McGinnis, *The Friendship Factor: How to Get Closer to the People You Care For* (Minneapolis: Augsburg, 1979), 70.
5. Email correspondence to me from Brian Reed on February 21, 2016. Used by permission.
6. Mark Rutland, *Streams of Mercy: Receiving and Reflecting God's Grace* (Ann Arbor, MI: Servant Publications, 1999), 39.

Chapter 9: Speak Up

1. W. E. Vine, *Vine's Expository Dictionary of New Testament Words: A Comprehensive Dictionary of the Original Greek Words with Their Precise Meanings for English Readers* (McLean, VA: MacDonald Publishing, n.d.), "Admonition, Admonish," 32.

Chapter 10: You've Been Bustered

1. "Peace of Mind," a sociological study conducted by Duke University, cited in Rudy A. Magnan, *Reinventing American Education: Applying Innovative and Quality Thinking to Solving Problems in Education* (Bloomington, IN: Xlibris, 2010), 23. These are the other four: 1. Staying involved with the living world. 2. Cultivating old-fashioned virtues: love, humor, compassion, and loyalty. 3. Not expecting too much of oneself. 4. Finding something bigger than oneself to believe in.
2. Charlotte vanOyen Witvliet, Thomas E. Ludwig, and Kelly L. Vander Laan, "Granting Forgiveness or Harboring Grudges: Implications for Emotion, Physiology, and Health," *Psychological Science* 12, no. 2 (March 2001): 117–23, https://greatergood.berkeley.edu/images/uploads/VanOyenWitvliet -GrantingForgiveness.pdf.

3. "John Wesley," Bible.org, https://bible.org/illustration/john-wesley-1.

4. Jayson Casper in Cairo, "Forgiving ISIS: Christian 'Resistance' Videos Go Viral in Arab World," ChristianityToday.com, March 17, 2015, http://www.christianitytoday.com/gleanings/2015/march/forgiving-isis-christian-resistance-viral-video-sat7-myriam.html.

Chapter 11: Be Loved, Then Love

1. Ian Fisher, "Fingers That Keep the Most Treasured Violins Fit," *New York Times*, June 3, 2007, https://www.nytimes.com/2007/06/03/world/europe/03cremona.html. See also Martin Gani, "The Violin-Makers of Cremona," *Italy Magazine*, January 20, 2012, http://www.italymagazine.com/featured-story/violin-makers-cremona.

2. W. E. Vine, *Vine's Expository Dictionary of New Testament Words: A Comprehensive Dictionary of the Original Greek Words with Their Precise Meanings for English Readers* (McLean, VA: MacDonald Publishing, n.d.), "Love," 702.

3. Vine, "Made," 709–10.

The Next Step

1. John Feinstein, "How Jake Olson of USC Became the Most Famous Long Snapper in College Football," *Washington Post*, September 5, 2017, https://www.washingtonpost.com/sports/colleges/how-jake-olson-of-usc-became-the-most-famous-long-snapper-in-college-football/2017/09/05/900672f0-923a-11e7-8754-d478688d23b4_story.html?utm_term=.0a4b2ae5befb.

Questions for Reflection

1. Bible Study Tools, s.v. "parakaleo," https://www.biblestudytools.com/lexicons/greek/nas/parakaleo.html.

2. Craig S. Keener, *The IVP Bible Background Commentary: New Testament* (Downers Grove, IL: InterVarsity, 1993), 448.

3. "3560. Noutheteó," Bible Hub, https://biblehub.com/greek/3560.htm.

4. Henri J. M. Nouwen, *Life of the Beloved: Spiritual Living in a Secular World* (New York: Crossroad Publishing, 1992), 77.

The Lucado Reader's Guide

Discover . . . Inside every book by Max Lucado, you'll find words of encouragement and inspiration that will draw you into a deeper experience with Jesus and treasures for your walk with God. What will you discover?

3:16: The Numbers of Hope
. . . the 26 words that can change your life.
core scripture: John 3:16

And the Angels Were Silent
. . . what Jesus Christ's final days can teach you about what matters most.
core scripture: Matthew 20–27

Anxious for Nothing
. . . be anxious for nothing.
core scripture: Philippians 4:4–8

The Applause of Heaven
. . . the secret to a truly satisfying life.
core scripture: The Beatitudes, Matthew 5:1–10

Before Amen
. . . the power of a simple prayer.
core scripture: Psalm 145:19

Come Thirsty
. . . how to rehydrate your heart and sink into the wellspring of God's love.
core scripture: John 7:37–38

Cure for the Common Life
. . . the unique things God designed you to do with your life.
core scripture: 1 Corinthians 12:7

Facing Your Giants
. . . when God is for you, no challenge is too great.
core scripture: 1 and 2 Samuel

Fearless
. . . how faith is the antidote to the fear in your life.
core scripture: John 14:1, 3

A Gentle Thunder
. . . the God who will do whatever it takes to lead his children back to him.
core scripture: Psalm 81:7

Glory Days
. . . how you fight from victory, not for it.
core scripture: Joshua 21:43–45

God Came Near
. . . a love so great that it left heaven to become part of your world.
core scripture: John 1:14

Grace
. . . the incredible gift that saves and sustains you.
core scripture: Hebrews 12:15

The Great House of God
. . . a blueprint for peace, joy, and love found in the Lord's Prayer.
core scripture: The Lord's Prayer, Matthew 6:9–13

He Chose the Nails
. . . a love so deep that it chose death on a cross—just to win your heart.
core scripture: 1 Peter 1:18–20

He Still Moves Stones
. . . the God who still does the impossible—in your life.
core scripture: Matthew 12:20

In the Eye of the Storm
. . . peace in the storms of your life.
core scripture: John 6

In the Grip of Grace
. . . the greatest gift of all—the grace of God.
core scripture: Romans

It's Not About Me
. . . why focusing on God will make sense of your life.
core scripture: 2 Corinthians 3:18

Just Like Jesus
. . . a life free from guilt, fear, and anxiety.
core scripture: Ephesians 4:23–24

A Love Worth Giving
. . . how living loved frees you to love others.
core scripture: 1 Corinthians 13

Next Door Savior
. . . a God who walked life's hardest trials—and still walks with you through yours.
core scripture: Matthew 16:13–16

No Wonder They Call Him the Savior
. . . hope in the unlikeliest place—upon the cross.
core scripture: Romans 5:15

Outlive Your Life
. . . that a great God created you to do great things.
core scripture: Acts 1

Six Hours One Friday
. . . forgiveness and healing in the middle of loss and failure.
core scripture: John 19–20

Traveling Light
. . . the power to release the burdens you were never meant to carry.
core scripture: Psalm 23

Unshakable Hope
. . . God has given us his very great and precious promises.
core scripture: 2 Peter 1:4

When God Whispers Your Name
. . . the path to hope in knowing that God knows you, never forgets you, and cares about the details of your life.
core scripture: John 10:3

You'll Get Through This
. . . hope in the midst of your hard times and a God who uses the mess of life for good.
core scripture: Genesis 50:20

Recommended reading if you're struggling with . . .

FEAR AND WORRY

Anxious for Nothing
Before Amen
Come Thirsty
Fearless
For the Tough Times
Next Door Savior
Traveling Light

DISCOURAGEMENT

He Still Moves Stones
Next Door Savior

GRIEF/DEATH OF A LOVED ONE

Next Door Savior
Traveling Light
When Christ Comes
When God Whispers Your Name
You'll Get Through This

GUILT

In the Grip of Grace
Just Like Jesus

LONELINESS

God Came Near

SIN

Before Amen
Facing Your Giants
He Chose the Nails
Six Hours One Friday

WEARINESS

Before Amen
When God Whispers Your Name
You'll Get Through This

Recommended reading if you want to know more about . . .

THE CROSS

And the Angels Were Silent
He Chose the Nails
No Wonder They Call Him the Savior
Six Hours One Friday

GRACE

Before Amen
Grace
He Chose the Nails
In the Grip of Grace

HEAVEN

The Applause of Heaven
When Christ Comes

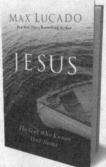

SHARING THE GOSPEL

God Came Near
Grace
No Wonder They Call Him the Savior

Recommended reading if you're looking for more . . .

COMFORT

For the Tough Times
He Chose the Nails
Next Door Savior
Traveling Light
You'll Get Through This

COMPASSION

Outlive Your Life

COURAGE

Facing Your Giants
Fearless

HOPE

3:16: The Numbers of Hope
Before Amen
Facing Your Giants
A Gentle Thunder
God Came Near
Grace
Unshakable Hope

JOY

The Applause of Heaven
Cure for the Common Life
When God Whispers Your Name

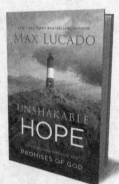

LOVE

Come Thirsty
A Love Worth Giving
No Wonder They Call Him the Savior

PEACE

And the Angels Were Silent
Anxious for Nothing
Before Amen
The Great House of God
In the Eye of the Storm
Traveling Light
You'll Get Through This

SATISFACTION

And the Angels Were Silent
Come Thirsty
Cure for the Common Life
Great Day Every Day

TRUST

A Gentle Thunder
It's Not About Me
Next Door Savior

Max Lucado books make great gifts!

If you're coming up to a special occasion, consider one of these.

FOR ADULTS:

Anxious for Nothing
For the Tough Times
Grace for the Moment
Live Loved
The Lucado Life Lessons Study Bible
Mocha with Max
DaySpring Daybrighteners® and cards

FOR TEENS/GRADUATES:

Let the Journey Begin
You Can Be Everything God Wants You to Be
You Were Made to Make a Difference

FOR KIDS:

I'm Not a Scaredy Cat
Just in Case You Ever Wonder
The Oak Inside the Acorn
You Are Special

FOR PASTORS AND TEACHERS:

God Thinks You're Wonderful
You Changed My Life

AT CHRISTMAS:

Because of Bethlehem
The Crippled Lamb
The Christmas Candle
God Came Near

ALSO AVAILABLE FROM MAX LUCADO

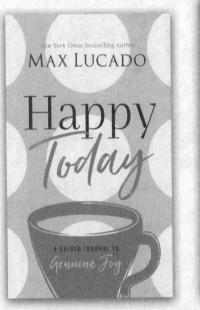

Happy Today is a 52-week companion journal to *How Happiness Happens*.

Each entry includes a short reading from Max, a Scripture, and a writing prompt with space for your own reflections and journaling.

New Video Study for Your Church or Small Group

If you've enjoyed this book, now you can go deeper with the companion video Bible study!

In this six-session study, Max Lucado helps you apply the principles in *How Happiness Happens* to your life. The study guide includes video notes, group discussion questions, and personal study and reflection materials for in-between sessions.

Study Guide
9780310105718

DVD
9780310105732

Available now at your favorite bookstore,
or streaming video on StudyGateway.com.

THOMAS NELSON
® *Since 1798*

Inspired by what you just read?

Connect with Max.

Listen to Max's teaching ministry, UpWords, on the radio and online. Visit www.MaxLucado.com to get FREE resources for spiritual growth and encouragement, including:

- Archives of *UpWords*, Max's daily radio program, and a list of radio stations where it airs
- Devotionals and e-mails from Max
- First look at book excerpts
- Downloads of audio, video, and printed material
- Mobile content

You will also find an online store and special offers.

www.MaxLucado.com

1-800-822-9673

UpWords Ministries
P.O. Box 692170
San Antonio, TX 78269-2170

Join the Max Lucado community:
Facebook.com/MaxLucado
Instagram.com/MaxLucado
Twitter.com/MaxLucado

Enjoy even more of Pastor Max Lucado's insights as he guides you through the Bible from Genesis to Revelation. Using his masterful storytelling gift, you'll be encouraged on your walk with God with lessons drawn from biblical characters, hundreds of notes that provide color and context to the Scripture, practical articles for growing in Christ, featured verses that remind you how much God cares for you, and plenty of room to journal your prayers and observations along the way.

DOWNLOAD THE BOOK OF ROMANS FREE

LUCADOENCOURAGINGWORD.COM

 THOMAS NELSON *Since 1798* NKJV NIV